Library Management in Disruptive Times

Skills and knowledge for an uncertain future

Every purchase of a Facet book helps to fund CILIP's advocacy, awareness and accreditation programmes for information professionals.

Library Management in Disruptive Times
Skills and knowledge for an uncertain future

Edited by
Steve O'Connor

facet publishing

Published by Facet Publishing,
7 Ridgmount Street, London WC1E 7AE
www.facetpublishing.co.uk

Facet Publishing is wholly owned by CILIP: the Chartered Institute of
Library and Information Professionals.

British Library Cataloguing in Publication Data
A catalogue record for this book is available from the British Library.

ISBN 978-1-78330-021-1

First published 2015

Text printed on FSC accredited material.

Typeset from editor's files by Facet Publishing Production in 10/14 pt
Century Schoolbook and Myriad Pro.

Printed and made in Great Britain by
CPI Group (UK) Ltd, Croydon, CR0 4YY.

Contents

Contributors

Choy Fatt Cheong

Choy Fatt Cheong is University Librarian at Nanyang Technological University (NTU). He began his career in librarianship at the National University of Singapore in 1984 and moved on to the Ministry of Defence in 1991 as Chief Librarian of SAFTI Military Institute. He was Principal Lecturer and Course Manager of Information Studies at Temasek Polytechnic from 1995 to 2000. He left the Polytechnic to set up his own consultancy and training company in 2000 and worked on various projects until 2004, when he assumed his current position. He also taught at the Division of Information Studies at NTU as Adjunct Associate Professor in 2003. He was President of the Library Association of Singapore from 1997 to March 2005 and served as a member of the Board of Directors at the Singapore National Library Board for six years until 2003. He is currently a board member of IATUL (the International Association of University Libraries) and leads several groups in the Library Association of Singapore (LAS) involving professional development, library education and a library executive management programme.

Bill Fisher

Bill Fisher is Professor with the School of Information at San Jose State University (SJSU) in California. He has been teaching in the library and information science (LIS) field for over 30 years; prior to joining SJSU, he taught at University of California Los Angeles; he has been a visiting professor at the University of British Columbia and is currently an adjunct professor at Queensland University of Technology. His teaching areas include administration/management, leadership, and organizational development, as well as resources/services in business/economics and sports/recreation. He has published on many aspects of management in libraries, including strategic alignment and the organizational impacts of change.

Daniel Forsman

Daniel Forsman is the Library Director at Chalmers University of Technology in Gothenburg, Sweden. Chalmers is a highly progressive university with a dynamic and ever-evolving library. Since 2010 the library has been using Scrum as an agile software development tool and has invested heavily in user experience (UX) methodology. Early in 2014 the library was reorganized, with the aim of introducing agile principles throughout the library organization, thus providing opportunities for all parts of the library to innovate and adapt to change.

Before becoming Director, Daniel managed many of the back-end operations of Chalmers Library, including library systems, cataloguing, inter-library loan, acquisitions, and web and social media presence. His first years in the profession were spent as a systems librarian, with a focus on library automation and the development of electronic services for libraries.

Sue Henczel

Sue Henczel is a library manager, practitioner, trainer and educator. Her areas of specialization include library metrics, information audit and professional associations. During her career she has held key roles within professional associations including Public Libraries Australia, the Special Libraries Association (SLA) and the Statistics and Evaluation Committee of the International Federation of Library Associations. Sue is an SLA Fellow and recipient of the 2008 Presidential Citation for services to the Association. She is a member of the Library Management (Emerald) Editorial Board and is its Book Review Editor.

Sue is currently a PhD candidate at RMIT University, Melbourne, where she is researching the impact of national library associations, and occasionally teaches on the Master of Information Management programme.

Petros A. Kostagiolas

Dr Petros A. Kostagiolas is Assistant Professor of Information Services Management in the Department of Archives, Library Science and Museology, Faculty of Information Science and Informatics at Ionian University, Corfu, Greece. He is also a visiting lecturer at Robert Gordon University, Aberdeen. He holds a PhD in the field of quality and reliability management from the University of Birmingham, UK, and he has published his work in international journals and conference proceedings. He has been co-author of four management books in Greek and is the author of a book in English published by Chandos-Elsevier. His research interests include the theory and practice of information services management, intellectual capital management, quality management, as well as information-seeking behaviour in various settings.

Steve O'Connor

Steve O'Connor is the Director of Information Exponentials. Steve's book on scenario planning for libraries and other organizations, *Imagining Your Library's Future*, is being published in Chinese by the National Library of China. He is the author of over 60 articles and a frequent presenter at international library and information management conferences. Most recently, he has been appointed as an Adjunct Professor at Charles Sturt University, where he engages in a variety of advisory and research roles. Steve's passion is to foster creative and dynamic communities that deliver positive and measureable results for their members. He has conducted scenario planning projects for many libraries and consortia, including for Lyrasis in its transformation from SOLINET into the largest library consortium in the USA. Steve has worked in libraries for most of his career. During the last 20 years, he has been University Librarian at two major academic libraries – University of Technology, Sydney, and Hong Kong Polytechnic University; CEO of CAVAL, a non-profit company providing a range of services to all library sectors; and founder of Information Exponentials. Steve harnesses the power of the imagination to create powerful, realistic and community-accepted future scenarios. He has conducted workshops on library futures and scenario planning across Australia and China and in Hong Kong, Singapore, Bangkok and Kuala Lumpur. Steve is the Editor of the journal *Library Management*.

Michael Robinson

Michael Robinson took up the position of Chief Executive Officer at the Australian library consortium CAVAL in September 2012. Prior to this he was Librarian at the Hong Kong Institute of Education, where he was actively involved in planning and implementing co-operative developments among Hong Kong university libraries with JULAC, the Joint University Librarians Advisory Committee. He was previously the Director of Library and Learning Resource Centre Projects for RMIT University Vietnam, undertaking major library building and infrastructure philanthropic projects for four Vietnamese universities, in addition to projects such as the authorized Vietnamese translation of the Dewey Decimal Classification (14th Abridged Edition) and programmes to support the re-establishment of the Vietnamese Library Association. He has been actively involved in library professional associations for many years, having been a member of the initial project development group and, subsequently, Core Trainer for the IFLA Building Strong Library Associations (BSLA) programme, conducting BSLA programmes in Vietnam, Nepal and Myanmar. He was the President of the Hong Kong Library Association from 2008 to 2009, and previously the President of VALA, the Victorian Association for Library Automation. Earlier in his career Michael was Associate University Librarian and Manager, Business Development, at RMIT University in Melbourne, Australia.

Ian Smith

Ian Smith is an Australian-based change management consultant and facilitator. He is an established and popular author on change and organizational improvement. Ian's writing strives to give managers and organizational leaders ideas and practical tools for grappling with the problems of effecting change with and through people.

Ian's career in the Australian higher education sector has spanned over 40 years, with four career switches: librarian, human resources manager; change manager, and independent consultant/facilitator/mediator. The service ethos inherent in the work of libraries and librarians has run through all of Ian's work, as has the capacity to work with and interpret complexity – this latter skill first learned as a reference librarian in pre-internet days.

Colin Storey

Dr Colin Storey, now retired to the leafy lanes of Suffolk, England, was the University Librarian of the Chinese University of Hong Kong from October 2000 to December 2012. He worked in academic libraries in the UK and in Hong Kong for 40 years.

Born in Liverpool, Colin received his BA (Leeds University, UK) and MPhil degrees (University of East Anglia, UK) in modern Chinese Studies. He moved to Hong Kong in 1988, as Associate Librarian at the Hong Kong Polytechnic University. He was awarded a PhD from the University of Hong Kong in 2000 for a thesis on information flow in academic libraries in the People's Republic of China, 1949–89.

Colin's professional interests include: academic library strategic management (particularly in times of economic stringency), personnel management and staff development, human interfaces with new technologies; intellectual property and copyright, and rare books. In retirement, Colin continues to struggle with mastering electric blues guitar and to sort out thousands of his books which have been in storage for 25 years.

Introduction

Steve O'Connor

As an accidental editor

As the editor of this volume, I sought chapters from a wide range of knowledgeable, influential and thoughtful contributors around the globe. They were each asked to write about the impact of 'disruptive change' on libraries, library management and library managers as they saw it. Each author has a particular area of expertise and perspective on that impact. I believe that the resulting volume offers perspectives on many aspects of library sectors, professional associations, geographic regions and education.

From my perspective as a journal editor, it is often absorbing to read and judge the many unsolicited articles received from fellow professionals. The journal articles are reflective of the issues that are on the minds of those who are leading the profession. Admittedly, the writers are not always in leadership roles, but they are influencing the thinking and management behaviours in the profession at all levels. Those that are published become part of the corpus of what is happening in the profession at that particular time.

The chapters of this volume, however, have been specifically commissioned. Many of the authors have published at one time or another in *Library Management* and elsewhere. But here they are writing to the brief 'What is the impact of disruption in libraries on your area of expertise?'

Ian Smith is an international authority on change management. His writings are sought after and his advice and insights are well received. His Chapter 1, on the five themes of change, is an excellent chapter with which to begin the discussion on disruption. Ian's experience is clearly articulated and highly readable.

Bill Fisher is a professor in the School of Library and Information Science at the San Jose State University. In Chapter 2 he discusses management fads and fashions and their impact on libraries. Bill is a highly experienced and insightful library academic working in the area of leadership and management. His starting point is that the current 'off the shelf' management theorem seems to provide the easy way forward. He argues that management is pure, hard work, especially in an environment where the only constant is change. He guides us to the areas we need to focus on in order to achieve good results while remaining wary that the fads and fashions may not deliver the easy, long-terms solutions that we hope for.

Choy Fatt Cheong is a highly experienced and perceptive university librarian based in Singapore. He is one of Asia's most knowledgeable librarians. It is perhaps understandable that he should have chosen Ranganathan's Five Laws of Library Science as the point of departure for his chapter. In Chapter 3 he develops a new set of Rules of User Engagement for libraries, extrapolated from Ranganathan but clearly shaped by the impact of the internet.

Michael Robinson, as the CEO of a large consortium company based in Melbourne, has brought a wealth of library experience in Vietnam, Hong Kong and Australia to his role. In Chapter 4 he argues that the value proposition of consortial activity, where costs and, especially, value are paramount, is becoming stronger. Michael demonstrates this value proposition across the range of library business offerings made by CAVAL.

Petros A. Kostagiolas is a professor at the Ionian University in Greece. In Chapter 5 he assesses the impact of the economic crisis in his own country and more broadly in Europe. He argues that the economic crisis has led to a new evaluation of decision-making processes in libraries. This includes evaluation of the value of public investment in libraries and the kinds of meta-marketing which should be undertaken.

Daniel Forsman is a university librarian in Sweden, and in Chapter 6 he looks at agile management techniques as a means to constantly re-evaluate priorities in libraries. As crises of identity, finance, management styles and acceptance of libraries become real, 'agile management' offers a different way forward.

Susan Henczel is a widely experienced librarian, author and academic with strong international connections. In Chapter 7 she writes about the role of the professional association in redefining the profession for sustainability in a disrupted world. Now that many librarians are working outside the traditional structures of the library, the challenge is that much greater. She highlights areas for development, even as the rate of participation in professional associations declines.

Colin Storey is a highly respected university librarian, recently retired. His perspective in Chapter 8 on the challenges facing current library management is very readable and nuanced. Colin has worked his way through all these disruptive changes, and at the same time engaged with Chinese cultures in Hong Kong and mainland China. Colin introduces us to ten pieces of advice for a satisfying and successful managerial career in libraries. His chapter is well worth reading.

Finally, in Chapter 9 Steve O'Connor discusses the meaning and impact of 'disruption', as defined by Christenson,[1] in the context of libraries and publishing. Having extensive library management, publishing and leadership experience, he makes the point that it is important to think outside the library literature and project your planning horizons into the world of what could be. This will help to shape future scenarios in the library environment.

I have had a great opportunity, as the editor of *Library Management*, to observe debates and developments in the broad world of library management. For me as a journal editor working with an experienced, senior and global editorial advisory board, the 'helicopter view' is privileged and equally global. Such a perspective sharpens one's awareness of the issues facing this sector of the profession. The subject focus of articles received from different areas of the globe ebbs and flows, depending on needs and developments in different arenas, and has changed quite significantly as libraries in Western countries come under increased financial and purposive pressures.

This volume gathers together a group of authors who, as library managers, operate in the maelstrom of change. I offer them my grateful thanks for writing for this volume. Each one has written with commitment and eloquence. As to you, the reader, I hope that you will profit from the variety of perspectives and advice within these pages and learn from them as you need. You may not agree with all that you read here, but it is hoped that a clearer articulation of your own position will emerge.

Steve O'Connor

Note

1   The most popular of Christenson's works is *The Innovator's Dilemma*, Harvard Business School Press, 1997.

CHAPTER 1

Leading change: knowledge for success

Ian Smith

Introduction

Library Management in Disruptive Times, the title of this book, brings to mind the (probably apocryphal) curse 'May you live in interesting times!' For libraries and librarians the current times, and those of the past several decades, have indeed been interesting and challenging. The advent and rapid growth of the internet has brought fundamental changes in information-seeking behaviours and has revolutionized the way in which libraries operate. As recently as the mid-1990s, libraries and librarians were the primary gateways and gatekeepers to information. Now they operate in circumstances where, if they are to remain relevant and viable, they have to embrace major change. Not to do so risks shrinking relevance – even redundancy. A conference held in 2006 in Hong Kong captured well the reality of this dynamic, posing the question: 'Are libraries and librarians like a dinosaur, or a phoenix? Will they die or will they fly?'

For managers of libraries to survive and prosper in disruptive times the capacity to lead, and to manage change is critical. If libraries are to be phoenix-like, to 'fly', they need to join into the flow of the massive disruptions brought about by new information technologies and changes in the information-seeking behaviours of library clients. They must be able to change. Survival will require innovation, diversification, flexibility and the capacity to keep on changing. Change can bring reinvention and new relevance. Failure to implement effective change carries the risk of, at best, mediocrity; more likely, a lingering decline into irrelevance. Failure to change, to remain relevant and valued by their clients, translates to a very real risk of redundancy, and the fate of the dinosaurs.

To survive and prosper, library managers need to know how to change. They need to recognize when change is needed, to be able to lead and sustain change, and to keep change alive and ongoing. The statistics on the effectiveness of change initiatives can, however, be disheartening. Estimates of the failure rate of organizational change initiatives, failure in full or in part, are as high as 70% (Kotter, 1995). However, despite those gloomy statistics, effective change *can* be achieved. Organizational change, led and managed well, provides an opportunity for growth, renewal and improved organizational capability. Change done well, that persists and leads to further innovation and improvement, can be revitalizing – for organizations and for those working in them. Conversely, change handled badly can create major and long-lasting organizational damage. People can be left disheartened, demoralized and cynical: people who, next time a 'change' initiative comes around, may well be wary – or, worse, obstructive. There is a lot at stake with change. There are strong reasons to manage change well; strong reasons to not get it wrong.

While there is no magic answer or solution to achieving change, there is much useful knowledge and guidance available. The discussion in this chapter considers several key aspects in the dynamics of change, providing a thought-starter for managers faced with the need to make change, and pointers to sources of more detailed advice and knowledge.

The discussion is arranged around five themes:

- ■ Change: it's all about people
- ■ Change: a step-by-step process, or a cycle?
- ■ Communication and engagement: keys to effective change
- ■ Resistance to change: opportunity or threat?
- ■ Keeping change alive: avoiding organizational homeostasis.

The chapter concludes with a reflection: is achieving change about managing, or leading? Or a mix of both?

Change: it's all about people

Transformation is impossible unless ... people are willing to help, often to the point of making short-term sacrifices. Employees will not make sacrifices if they are happy with the status quo, unless they believe that useful change is possible.

(Kotter, 1995)

Organizations are made up of people. It is the people who either will embrace change and carry it forward or will block and undermine change. The way in which people are led and managed during change is key in determining the path to success or to failure of any initiative for change.

For some, change is hugely exciting. For others, deeply frightening. To make change happen it is essential to engage people in the change. Other than in an emergency, simply directing change to occur and imposing change rarely succeeds. It may appear on the surface that the change has worked. Indeed some of the change may stick. Change that is simply imposed without real engagement and buy-in from the people involved is, however, at best, likely to be seriously compromised. At worst, it may leave major organizational damage, eroding, even destroying, trust in the organization's leadership. This can lead to a worsening of already poor circumstances – making future change even harder to achieve. Establishing a solid support base for organizational changes and undertaking ongoing active enlistment to the change effort is vital. As John Kotter says, capturing the hearts and minds of the people who make up the organization is key to achieving successful and enduring change.

Philosopher Jonathan Haidt (2006) has a good analogy for human behaviour when faced with change. He says that our emotional side is an elephant and our rational side is its rider. Perched atop the elephant, the rider holds the reins, appearing to be the leader and directing the elephant where to go. However, the reality is that the rider's control is precarious. The rider is very small relative to the elephant. The analytical, logical rider may decide on the way to go and direct that action. However, the reality is that in any disagreement over where to go, the rider is very likely to lose. So it is with organizational change. Organizations can be like very large and wilful 'elephants'. If they do not want to change, or to change in the way directed by the rider (the leader/manager), then real change is very unlikely. No matter how much the rider shouts and prods, in a contest of wills the elephant is very likely to be the ultimate winner. What is required is a more nuanced approach, whispering to achieve change rather than directing change through a megaphone.

Chip and Dan Heath (2010) take Haidt's analogy and expand the concept in their best-selling and insightful analysis of the task of achieving change: *Switch: how to change things when change is hard*. Using the image of the rider on the elephant, the Heaths argue that achieving change is about doing three things well:

- directing the rider – not the elephant
- motivating the elephant to change – rather than simply directing it to change
- shaping the path – to make change easier for the elephant

If you can do all three of these at the same time, then, say the Heaths, dramatic change can happen.

The Heaths' concepts provide simple but powerful tools to apply to the task of achieving organizational change, achieving change with and through people. To briefly expand on the Heaths' model (read the book if you want to know more), the three steps involve the elements described here.

Direct the rider (not the elephant)

Follow the bright spots in an organization. Instead of starting from scratch, find out what's working, find the points of common ground (both good and bad). Investigate what is working well and clone it. Search out the negatives – those things that are not working well – and use those as hooks to engage people in working for improvement.

Script critical moves in the change. Don't simply think and articulate the big picture. That is important, but in order to connect with people and to make their part in the change real and tangible it is necessary to think in terms of specific behaviours and actions. So explain these to people, and engage them in the action.

Point to the destination. It is much easier for people to embrace change if they know where they are going. Do this in a way that makes sense to them and their role in the organization. People will accept and join in with change when they know where it is taking them, and why it's worth it to go there.

Motivate the elephant

Find and work with people's feelings in the change. Simply knowing the logic of the change is generally not enough to cause people to change. The key to change is finding a way to get people to feel something about the change. So, instead of an approach of analyse/think/change, try approaching change from a standpoint of see/feel/change.

Shrink the change. It is easier for people to make a change if the change seems doable, rather than insurmountable. Break down the change until it no longer spooks the elephant. Look for quick wins in making change, which can then build momentum towards more change.

Grow people. Cultivate a sense of identity in people and instil a change mind-set. The Heaths argue that most people have a pre-existing inclination towards the 'bright spots'. This is despite the fact that it is a frequent human tendency to focus more on what is bad than on what is good. People will generally respond well to a challenge to find what is working well and to do more of it. Focusing on what is working well (the bright spots) is more motivating than a focus on what is not working well (even though the latter has the intent of improvement). So, get people to start thinking that change really is possible and that it is worthwhile. Get them to make a small change and to see the results. They can then think of themselves as people who *can* change, rather than people who are limited by habit, peer pressure etc. and who cannot change.

Shape the path

Tweak the environment. Adjusting and aligning the environment to make the desired changes easier does just that – it makes the changes easier. It also makes going against the changes a harder option. The elephant will take the easiest path, and will likely baulk at a harder path – even if it is directed to take that path. So make the path of change that you want to be followed as easy and as smooth as you can.

Build habits. When behaviour is habitual, it is easy to just keep
  following the same path. People tend to be habitual, and following
  the easy and known path does not tax the rider. Look for ways to set
  and embed habits that fit with and encourage the change. Look for
  ways to discourage habits that run counter to the desired change.
Rally the herd. Behaviour is contagious. People watch other people, and
  they copy and follow behaviours that they see – good or bad. So, to
  foster change and help it spread, rally the proponents and the
  exemplars of change and allow them to shine – showing others what
  can be and is being achieved. Pretty soon more and more people will
  join in and the momentum for change will build.

The Heaths' analysis, which is at heart about the behaviours of people
when faced with change, offers a powerful but simple model for working
to achieve change. Their book finishes with a reflection on keeping change
going. This may sound easy, but it is not. This topic will be considered
further, later in this chapter.

Change: a step-by-step process, or a cycle?

John P. Kotter, of the Harvard Business School, has been a highly
influential observer and analyst of organizational change over many years.
His classic analysis of the sequence of effective change is essentially that
of a series of steps – each critical to effective change, and each of which
must be done in sequence. Kotter's seminal analysis (1995) was drawn from
his observation of over a hundred companies, large and small, attempting
to reinvent themselves, with varying degrees of success. Done well, Kotter
says, these eight steps provide the path to success. If done badly, or not
done at all, he says, they can be the root cause of change failure.

   In outline, Kotter's approach to achieving successful change is as
follows.

■ **Establish a sense of urgency about the need to achieve
   change.**
   People will not change if they cannot see the need to do so.
■ **Create a guiding coalition.**
   Assemble a group with power, energy and influence in the
   organization to lead the change.

- **Develop a vision and strategy.**
  Create a vision of what the change is about; tell people why the change is needed and how it will be achieved.
- **Communicate the change vision.**
  Tell people, in every possible way and at every opportunity, about the why, what and how of the changes.
- **Empower broad-based action.**
  Involve people in the change effort; get people to think about the changes and how to achieve them rather than thinking about why they do not like the changes and how to stop them.
- **Generate short-term wins.**
  Seeing the changes happening, and working and recognizing the work being done by people towards achieving the change, is critical.
- **Consolidate gains and produce more change.**
  Create momentum for change by building on successes in the change; invigorate people through the changes; develop people as change agents.
- **Anchor new approaches in the corporate culture.**
  This is critical to long-term success and institutionalizing the changes. Failure to do so may mean that changes achieved through hard work and effort slip away with people's tendency to revert to the old and comfortable ways of doing things.

Contrasting with Kotter's step-wise model of the dynamics of change is Bob Doppelt's (2003) analysis of change, drawn from wide-ranging and long-term observation of a mix of private and public sector organizations. Differing from Kotter's linear-step analysis, Doppelt views the process of change as a cycle or a 'wheel of change' (Figure 1.1).

Doppelt sees change as a messy and far from linear process. He articulates seven cycle points at which interventions may be made, or leverage applied, to effect change. Significantly, Doppelt's analysis is that, provided that all steps are ultimately carried through, interventions may be made at any point or in any sequence in the change cycle, and with varying degrees of attention or action. In Doppelt's observation, multiple and non-sequential interventions and actions build momentum for change. The seven intervention or leverage points in Doppelt's 'wheel of change' are explained below in more detail.

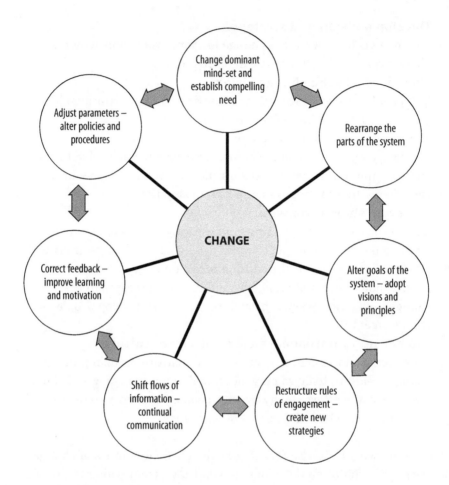

Figure 1.1 *Doppelt's 'wheel of change' (Doppelt, 2003)*

■ *Disrupt and change the dominant mind-set – establish a compelling need for achieving change.*
Disrupting an organization's controlling mental models is, in Doppelt's view, the first and most important step toward developing new ways of operating. Little change will occur if this step is unsuccessful.

■ *Rearrange the parts of the system by organizing transition teams.*
Having challenged and disrupted 'business-as-usual' thinking, rearrange the parts of the current system. Involve – in analysis, planning and implementation – people from as many functions, departments and levels of the organization as possible, along with

key external stakeholders. Shaking-up the organization is important in achieving change. People, from planners and decision makers to operational staff, tend to handle problems in the same way time after time. Loosening the constraints imposed by prevailing and dominant cultural paradigms encourages new ideas and action to emerge, at all levels of an organization.

- *Alter the goals of the system – create an ideal vision.*
  Changing organizational goals, and clearly articulating a vision of the ends the organization seeks to achieve, can change the first-order principles that guide decision making. This can enable different kinds of decisions and outcomes.

- *Restructure the rules of engagement – adopt new strategies.*
  The rules determining how work gets done must be altered after the organization has adopted and articulated revised purposes and goals. This may involve new tactics, and implementation plans. These changes need to occur at both operational and policy/governance levels.
  This stage, and the stage of altering the goals (above), requires organizations to consider:
  — what is the current state?
  — how and where does the organization want to be in the future?
  — how does the organization get there?
  — how do we measure progress?

- *Shift the flows of information – communicate vision, strategies and actions.*
  This is important in ensuring understanding and buy-in to change from staff and other stakeholders. Even when all other interventions have been successful, progress may stall without consistent exchange of clear information about the purpose, strategies and benefits of the change effort. Transparent communication opens the door to honest understanding and sharing.

- *Correct feedback loops in the organization – encourage and reward learning and innovation.*
  Improving feedback and learning mechanisms is key. Employees and stakeholders should be encouraged and enabled to continually expand their skills, knowledge and understanding. Changing that aspect of organizational functioning meshes with moving away from traditional feedback systems – typically oriented toward

maintaining the status quo – and towards mechanisms that foster innovation, experimentation and risk taking.
- *Adjust and align the parameters of the system.*
  Align internal systems, structures, policies and procedures with organizational goals in order to constantly reaffirm all of the required actions and behaviours.

Although Kotter and Doppelt differ in their view of the importance of sequential action, they both emphasize common core themes:

- Establish a sense of urgency about the need to change.
- Disrupt set ways of working and business-as-usual mind-sets.
- Create a vision of the ideal future state and then engage people in the organization with that change agenda and with actions to achieve the change.
- Communicate that change vision widely and consistently, and do so at all levels of the organization.
- Empower people in the organization to think and act differently, to take risks, to explore new ways of working and to overcome barriers to innovation and individual/organizational learning.
- Enable feedback loops in the organization, recognizing success in achieving change, which in turn encourages more change. This establishes an exponential and dynamic cycle that builds on success.
- Institutionalize new and changed approaches to working – embedding change and making it stick.

An overriding common view from both writers is that change processes take time – years of work – to achieve success. In Kotter's words, it is important to avoid the 'illusion of speed'. The key difference between them is that Kotter asserts the primacy of each step occurring in strict sequence, whereas Doppelt's view is that, while there is a strong element of logical flow in these change interventions, most situations allow for interventions to occur in a variety of sequences and with varying emphases. The Kotter and the Doppelt analyses of the dynamics of change both provide strong understanding of the complexities of the task of working to achieve change. A situational response that melds elements of both of these approaches may be the path to success.

Communication and engagement: keys to effective change

In all of the discussion above, in the analyses of Haidt, the Heaths, Kotter and Doppelt, the common element is the importance of the people who staff organizations and their behaviours in circumstances of change. A critical element in working with people and change is communication. Effective communication – honest, credible, agile and interactive communication – sits at the very core of good change management. It can be the critical enabler in moving beyond middling (or even failed) attempts at change, to a change strategy that is truly transformative and becomes embedded in the organization.

Good communication about change, while it may appear to be easy, is actually one of the hardest things to get right. The key to getting it right is, again, people. Engaging with people, understanding different audiences, communicating with them, enlisting them in the change – these are critical success factors. Engaging people, rather than simply talking at them or directing and imposing change, is essential. Yet the game plan for organizational change so often ignores this truth.

There are some basics of good change communication. Barbara LeTourneau – a health-care professional – developed a communication model that has much to recommend it for use in organizational change (LeTourneau, 2004). Her change communication 'prescription' has four key elements:

- engage
- empathize
- educate
- enlist.

Engage

Other than in an emergency, real change cannot be simply imposed. Genuine and thorough engagement with employees and stakeholders is required to achieve deeply embedded change. This should begin early in any change initiative and continue alongside change progress and not be seen as an afterthought, just as the change is about to be launched. Engaging employees and stakeholders early introduces and socializes the notion of change, actively generates interest and discussion about the changes and provokes responses to the change proposals. Responses will most likely cover the full range from positivity and enthusiasm for change to deep anxiety and resistance. And, unfortunately, a too-common managerial response to change resistance is to ignore, dismiss or squash such comment. While listening and responding to resistance may seem counter-intuitive, it is actually a powerful means of engagement. People rarely resist change simply for the sake of resisting; there is usually a deeper imperative. It is inevitable that negativity about at least some aspects of a change proposal will emerge. As much as it is important to listen to positive and supportive comment, and to encourage and cultivate support, it is equally important to listen to and engage with the anxiety and the resistance. The role of leaders and managers is to provide an opportunity for stakeholders to air their reactions and sentiments openly, and to do so sooner rather than later. (The issue of dealing with change resistance is discussed further, later in this chapter.)

Good engagement requires honest and straightforward explanations of the why and the how of the change. A mix of communication methods is important: large-scale 'big picture' messages from the organization's leaders play an important role, as do practical, grass-roots explanations of how change may impact on individuals and work groups. Consistent change messages must be developed and agreed – and team leaders and line managers need to be part of this consistent change message from the outset of the engagement phase. Change champions – those employees who will, from whatever position they occupy in the organization, develop (and encourage in others) ideas, energy and enthusiasm about change – often emerge during the engagement phase and they can become powerful ongoing advocates for change.

Empathize

Genuine and responsive listening is key to empathetic change communication. Acknowledgement, engagement with and due consideration of the issues and concerns raised is key. Some concerns may seem small in the scale of whole-of-organization change plans. However, they will be meaningful to whoever has raised them. On examination they may have wider relevance and importance – or they may not. While not all concerns can be solved to the satisfaction of those who raised them, what is important is listening to and considering what is said.

Legitimate concerns should be acted on wherever possible, and due credit should be given to those raising them. If people feel confident about making comments and raising concerns, and feel that they are being listened to and their comments are being considered, they are more likely to accept change, even if that change goes contrary to their ideas. Through genuine listening and empathy, change leaders can build confidence in the capacity of the organization to find and implement the right solutions to organizational challenges.

Educate

Educating people about a programme of changes is key and has to be done broadly and often. Simply because a leader has said that a change is to happen, it cannot be assumed that that is it. Leaders need to restate the change message, explaining the why and the how, again and again, in different venues, in different modes and with different people.

Leaders need to develop their own strategic approach to change communication that suits both their personal style and their organization's needs. Anyone can develop a PowerPoint presentation, plan a talk for a 'town hall' or small group meeting, or write an update bulletin or all-staff e-mail. But only a few do it well. Even fewer do it with effective strategic intent and impact. What looks easy is not. Tactics live and die in the shadow of strategy. Communication should include big-picture briefings by change leaders; interactive town-hall-style meetings of staff; team and group meetings; one-to-one meetings; and formal and informal exchanges, written, verbal and in all media. As stated above, communication and education about change must be a two-way process. Information should be imparted about the reasons for, and the nature of, change and there should be genuine exchange of questions, responses, reactions. This is the path to insights for all parties to the change.

As with engagement, education about change should begin early. Managers often think they should hold back on providing information about change until their ideas are more concrete. They may be concerned that releasing early and unformed information may stir worries and galvanize opposition to change. But the reality is that there is no perfect moment to announce a change. While judgement is required to avoid unsettlement by floating vague and unrealized ideas, unsettlement will happen whenever change plans are announced. And, equally, there will be excitement about the change on the part of many.

Open and early discussion about changes, education about the need for change and inviting reactions, ideas and responses to proposals for change can yield multiple benefits. Allowing worries and negative reactions to be aired and to run their course early in the change process means that these matters can be identified early and brought out into the open. Group attention can be applied to addressing such matters. Honesty and genuine engagement on the part of change managers develops trust and confidence on the part of employees. That trust is critical to developing and sustaining a strong support base for achieving enduring change.

Enlist

Enlisting people to the change effort develops the support base for change. To cite John Kotter once again:

> Without credible communication, and a lot of it, the hearts and minds of the troops are never captured.
>
> (Kotter, 2002)

Effective communication by the change leaders and managers works at all points on the response continuum. It engages the energy of the early adopters who want to know how, where and when. It gives time to the cautious employees who need space to gather insights and accurate information in order to work through their questions and concerns. With all of these people, communication – persistent and consistent – is vital in the (often drawn out) process of enlisting support. All points on the spectrum will be present in any organization – from those who can barely wait for change to start, to the residual cynics and chronic change resisters. They all need to be engaged – and credible, authentic communication is the key to engagement.

Communication – honest, open and two-way – is always an important element in the management of people. During times of organizational change, when employees are exposed to the upheaval of the old order and a change to the new, effective communication is even more important. And yet it is so often an afterthought. Authentic communication guided by simple principles of engagement, empathy, education and enlistment can go a long way to improving efforts to achieve change. Thinking change? Think communication – authentic, early and often.

Resistance to change: opportunity or threat?

People don't resist change. They resist being changed.

(Senge et al., 1999)

Resistance to change is normal. It should be expected as part of any change programme. Just as some people will embrace change, others will react differently and will resist change in varying degrees and ways. Resistance may be loud, active and open, or passive, quiet and undermining. The latter is the 'resistance which does not resist'. Although less obvious, passive resistance can be the most difficult to counter. Quiet rebuilding of organizational 'silos'; passively avoiding recognition and action on changes in structures, roles and reporting relationships; encouraging 'them and us' thinking; reversion to old ways of working; simple non-engagement with new ways of working – all are examples of passive or low-key resistance to change. Whatever form it takes, resistance can act as a powerful drag on momentum towards achieving change. Resistance should be expected, planned for and actively responded to. Just *how* to respond is the question. Should people resisting change be removed, ignored or engaged? Views differ on this point. As with any aspect of working with change, a situational and flexible response is most likely to succeed.

At one end of the response spectrum is the view that those resisting change are in essence a negative force and potentially powerful in influencing others against change. This analysis views change resisters as blockers. To allow these people attention and audience, so the argument goes, is not only a waste of time but dangerous. Allowing them to express their opposition risks the opposers gathering people to their cause and undermining the change effort. The solution: remove them; get rid of them from the organization, as they will never change. While removing them may result in short-term organizational damage, such as increased fear of and negativity towards the managers responsible for their removal, any damage will be short lived and the benefits will outweigh the negatives.

A less extreme version of that philosophy argues for simply ignoring those who oppose change. Ignore them and they will become marginalized and not listened to. Their opposition will become irrelevant, leaving them to either join the change or leave of their own volition.

Another option, one which may initially seem counter-intuitive, comes from a more nuanced understanding of the dynamics of change. In this analysis, resistance to change is seen as a significant opportunity. Manifest resistance to change shows that people *do* think and *do* care about how things are run in the organization. That care may seem to be misdirected, but it is better than apathy. There is much to be learned from giving resisters enough – but not too much – air time. Engaging with resistance provides the opportunity and the possibility to learn from that resistance; opportunity, potentially, to change the resistance into support. Understanding and considering the reasons for resistance may point to unseen flaws in the change proposals. In following this path when dealing with resistance, the questions 'why' and 'how' become powerful tools. Asking 'Why do you oppose this change?' and 'How would you do it differently?', engaging with resistance and concern about changes, can yield powerful knowledge for leaders and managers, and an understanding of where and why the resistance exists. Engaging with resistance also shows that leaders and managers *do* listen and *do* consider legitimate those views about the changes. Change resisters can be influential in bringing others over to their view. They can be even more powerful if they are seen to be being listened to and considered, being given a voice and input to determine both the direction and the strategy of change. A resister who becomes a change advocate can be a powerful ally in the change initiative.

This latter view of and approach to dealing with resistance to change is seated in a psycho-social understanding of organizational management, in trying to understand opposition to change, rather than in simply seeking to overcome it. This approach fits in with the Heaths' model of the nuanced direction of the rider. The 'get rid of the opposition' mind-set, while it may seem attractive as a quick fix, risks falling into the trap of directing the elephant – only to have the elephant become even more stubborn, and presenting a bigger problem further along the path to change. While it may take longer to engage and understand resistance to change, this approach can yield significantly better organizational outcomes. A nuanced, rather than a simply blunt, response to resistance offers the potential for a healthier organizational outcome in the long term.

All of that said, sometimes strong action will be required in dealing with resistance. While it is important to listen to critics and gainsayers, if the energy directed towards this becomes excessive, it may come at the expense of moving ahead and working with those people who are eager to progress change. While it is important to take the resistance seriously, engage with it and argue the case for change, leaders and managers should not waste time in trying to change the unchangeable. Some resistance and resisters to change will never go away. There comes a time when the correct response, after having engaged with and listened to resistance and resisters, is to move on with the change. To do otherwise is to risk sending a message to the resisters that if they just keep up the resistance they will get their way. Firm and honest action by managers to listen to and consider concerns, and then to decide on a way forward, engenders confidence in the willingness and ability of the managers to manage. Conversely, a weak or confused response can seriously compromise a change initiative.

As Peter Senge says, people don't resist change. What they resist is *being* changed. Wherever possible, try to engage and involve – don't just steam-roll the change. But be prepared for tough action in the face of resistance, if and when that is required.

Keeping change alive: avoiding organizational homeostasis

Imagine a balloon filled with air. When you press your finger into the side of the balloon the shape changes. When you remove your finger the balloon reverts to the original shape. In physics this is known as homeostasis – the tendency of a system to remain stable and, if changed, to return to the stable (pre-change) state. Organizations can be like a balloon: as soon as the pressure to change backs off, there is a risk that the organization will revert to the pre-change state. Getting change to stick and take root can be even harder than the original work to make the change happen.

Organizational culture eats strategy for breakfast – and for lunch and dinner too! The best laid plans and strategies for change can come to nothing if organizational culture – the norms, practices and shared values that influence the way in which the organization operates – does not mesh with and support the changes. Changes, especially if they run counter to the established organizational culture, can be very difficult to engrain and embed. The tendency to homeostasis can be a strong force.

To return to the earlier discussion and the analyses of John Kotter and Bob Doppelt, both argue that action to disrupt dominating mind-sets and ways of thinking and doing is critical. Doppelt (2003) says that the change effort never actually ends, that change is iterative and that the cycle of change needs to be kept in perpetual motion. In his view, the process of generating new knowledge, by both individual employees and the organization as a whole, leads to constantly new ways of thinking and acting. In this analysis key elements of organizational practice interact to achieve continuous reinforcement and strengthening of new ways of working. Kotter (1995) observes that cultural change comes out of, and not as a precursor to, effective change. True and lasting cultural change cannot be simply directed by the change leaders – no matter how strongly they try. In the Heaths' terms, the rider cannot simply direct the elephant to adopt a new organizational culture, mind-set and way of working. That has to be drawn out of the organization, reinforced, embedded and kept alive and nimble – lest the new culture become stale, lacking the capacity for critical review.

Borrowing from both Kotter and Doppelt, here are some useful general rules for making change stick and establishing a culture for sustained and persisting organizational change:

- Understand that cultural change comes last in the process of change – not first.
- Recognize that not everyone will come along with the changes, nor all at the same rate.
- Show and prove that new ways of doing things are better than the old ways.
- Make success visible and prominent; strengthen the new ways of working.
- Reinforce new norms, celebrate achievement and encourage a mind-set of continual critical review and improvement.
- Above all, keep the change alive and ongoing; avoid the 'balloon effect'.

Leading change or managing change? Whatever the case, make change happen!

Organizational behaviour guru Charles Handy has this to say about change:

> To 'manage change' is wishful thinking, implying as it does that one not only knows where to go and how to get there, but can persuade everyone else to travel there.

To 'cultivate change' is something different, suggesting an attitude of growth, of channelling rather than controlling, of learning not instruction. A changing organisation is one that uses differences to grow better.

(Handy, 1996)

Handy describes the dynamics of change well. Change does not happen by itself – nor is the process simple. While there is a strong element of management involved in managing the process and the stages of change, achieving successful change is a lot about guiding and steering, cultivating and leading change.

This chapter began by reflecting on the challenge that faces librarians and libraries: either to recognize and adapt to the need to change or to stick with tried and tested ways and, in doing so, risk ultimate irrelevance. For managers of libraries in disruptive times, change and adaptation is an imperative, not a choice. The imperative is to recognize the need for change, to establish a compelling story for change, and to show the pathway to change.

At the same Hong Kong conference noted at the start of this chapter, one speaker quoted a Chinese proverb, the essence of which is that no matter how sweet the soup is, if the road to the kitchen serving the soup is too long or bumpy, customers will go elsewhere. So it is for libraries. Libraries and librarians must learn to change, and to keep on changing, in response to the needs of their customers. Without effective change they risk irrelevance and redundancy. Without change, their customers will go elsewhere and be their customers no more. Learn to achieve successful change and be a phoenix. Fail in that learning, and a dinosaur's fate beckons.

References

Doppelt, B. (2003) *Leading Change Toward Sustainability: a change-management guide for business, government and civil society*, Greenleaf Publishing.

Haidt, J. (2006) *The Happiness Hypothesis*, Basic Books.

Handy, C. (1996) *Beyond Certainty: the changing worlds of organisations*, Harvard Business School Press.

Heath, C. and Heath, D. (2010) *Switch: how to change things when change is hard*, Broadway Books.

Kotter, J. P. (1995) Why Transformation Efforts Fail, *Harvard Business Review*, **73** (2), 12–20.

Kotter, J. P. (2002) *The Heart of Change: real-life stories of how people change their organisations*, Harvard Business School Press.

Senge, P. et al. (1999) *The Dance of Change: the challenges of sustaining momentum in learning organisations*, Nicholas Brealey.

Further reading

There is a large literature on change management. The references above and the list below are by no means exhaustive. Rather, they are sources that the author has found useful and that may provide a starting point for managers wishing to explore further the challenges of undertaking organizational change.

Change Management Institute (2013) *The Effective Change Manager: the change management body of knowledge*, Change Management Institute.

Hiatt, J. M. (2006) *ADKAR: a model for change in business, government and our community*, Prosci Learning Center.

Kotter, J. P. (1996) *Leading Change*, Harvard Business School Press.

LeTourneau, B. (2004) Communicate for Change, *Journal of Healthcare Management*, **49** (6), 354–7.

Miller, D. (2011) *Successful Change: how to implement change through people*, Changefirst.

Patterson, K. et al. (2008) *Influencer: the power to change anything*, McGraw-Hill.

CHAPTER 2

Management fads and fashions and their impact on the LIS community

Bill Fisher

Introduction

Anyone who has anything to do with managing an organization (or some part of an organization) knows that the first decade (plus) of the 21st century has brought a number of challenges that any organization and those responsible for making it function have had to face. And it appears that our reward for successfully navigating thus far is more of the same – both continuing, as well as new challenges to be faced in the years ahead.

What does this specifically mean for libraries? In March 2014 I put this question out to the discussion list of the Leadership and Management Division (LMD) of the Special Libraries Association, asking the members of this group to identify the major challenges they would face over the next five to six years. Within a couple of days a number of insightful responses had been posted to the LMD list identifying several key areas of concern:

- As expected, dealing with change was mentioned by a number of respondents. While we have a tendency to view change as disruptive and painful, we need to adopt a different point of view that allows us to see change as an opportunity that we can take advantage of to provide new or different services/resources, enhance our roles within our organizations and the like.
- Managing the expectation of our organizations by providing value based on what our customers want, not on what we may think they

want, was highly stressed.

- ▨ Leveraging this value we can position ourselves to deal with competition from others (both internally and externally) who feel they can do our jobs and/or feel we are no longer needed (e.g. the 'it's all free on the internet' mentality).
- ▨ One way to help make this happen is to collaborate with the right stakeholders, using clear and comprehensive communication.
- ▨ This becomes possible when we identify and develop leaders who understand the internal and external environments in which their organizations operate.

While these brief summaries capture much of the overall tone and direction of the responses, a couple of specific responses provided a slightly different viewpoint. Lori Zipperer, who has her own business, Zipperer Project Management, offered this view:

> Until we approach challenges, opportunities and day to day functionality through the appropriate organization lens (simple, complicated, complex) we are apt to design programs, services and the other structures through which to manage our workforce that set them up for failure. Managing complexity takes time and patience to identify and fix latent problems with a systems orientation, rather than a powerpoint [sic] 'off the shelf' mentality.
>
> (L. Zipperer, personal communication, 11 March 2014)

Another contributor to the discussion, Constance Ard, reinforced this approach, especially as it deals with technology, by adding: 'Technology continues to force evolutions and managers must challenge the "adopt all" mind-set and become more strategic about what they choose to consider, test, pilot and eventually implement' (C. Ard, personal communication, 11 March 2014).

These perspectives from Zipperer and Ard imply the need for a new approach to how we manage our organizations, and one more contributor, Chris Olsen, summed it up nicely: 'I think the challenge for info/km [knowledge management] managers through 2020 will be to recalibrate management styles and skills to match and lead scenarios we are starting to see surface' (C. Olsen, personal communication, 11 March 2014).

Change, change and more change

None of these contributions to the online discussion is particularly startling, certainly for anyone who pays more than a passing interest to our professional literature. Countless books, articles, reports and white papers have been written, presentations made, workshops held, and now webinars conducted, that have sought to identify (and sometimes solve) management challenges facing the library profession. Some of these are 'universal' challenges – those facing any library and information science (LIS) professional anywhere. Other contributors to the discussion take a more geographical approach and focus on challenges that may be specific to certain countries or regions. Yet others take an environmental approach and look at challenges for public libraries, for academic libraries, for archives, etc.

A problem one quickly identifies in using an approach to survey the recent literature is the difficulty of finding something that fits into *only one* of identified categories. Even when an author is trying to address a general or universal issue, they typically write from the perspective of a specific environment and/or location. That said, we can review a representative sample of recent works that adhere somewhat closely to these approaches.

Challenges for services and users

Derek Law (2011), in a paper presented at the 2011 International Federation of Library Associations and Institutions (IFLA) conference, sees a major challenge in providing services and collections relevant to the varied needs of a library's customers, which will necessitate changing the services and content we have to offer. He provides examples from both Europe and North America of projects that attempt to gather information on the effectiveness of new services and new content, so library decision makers will have evidence to assist them in providing the appropriate skills/knowledge for those working in libraries to ensure that the appropriate changes are identified and implemented.

Another perspective on how libraries need to address the challenge of change comes from three Nigerian authors (Adeyoyin, Imam and Bello, 2012). They support the idea that change is typically addressed from either a Newtonian perspective or a quantum perspective. Those taking a Newtonian approach view any organization as having separate working parts, such that as change occurs or is anticipated one focuses on the part of the organization that may be impacted upon and makes adjustments or tweaks as needed. The quantum approach recognizes that while changes may have an immediate impact on just one part of the organization, a more holistic view is necessary so as to deal with a 'wave effect' that eventually impacts on other parts of the organization, if not the entire enterprise. We've certainly seen this in the LIS field with the impact of technology. Library 'automation' initially was contained behind the scenes in our cataloguing operations, helping us to produce the cards in the catalogues that our customers would search. For the most part, only the cataloguing/technical services department was involved and the rest of us went about our business as usual – very Newtonian. Later, we were able to use technology to search for information (or, more accurately, representation of the information, since it was all bibliographic data at that time) and our reference/public services departments got involved; or at least, the one or two people who received the necessary training from Dialog or SDC Database Services did so, and the rest of us went about our business as usual. With the advent of OPACs (online public access catalogues) and the development of technology for our customers' direct use in accessing information, the first hint of a 'white cap' could be seen on the horizon, and that 'wave' is still impacting upon libraries today.

Thomas Frey, a futurist with the DaVinci Institute, has studied libraries for some time. Frey (2009) notes that, despite the predictions of libraries becoming irrelevant owing to the increased digitization of information, libraries (and his focus here is on public libraries) are experiencing renewed popularity because they have kept their collections and services relevant to the communities they serve. However, Frey does see the role of print/ink-on-paper books diminishing, which will result in 'bookless' libraries. This will present challenges for libraries to stay connected to their communities and to continue to be seen as relevant.

Challenges for different types of libraries

We can also look at some of the challenges facing the profession by environment or 'type' of library, although issues that were at one time unique to a public library or an academic library are becoming blurred as all libraries/information centres find themselves facing similar concerns. Nor are these concerns limited to a specific country or region. Jochumsen,

Rasmussen and Skot-Hansen (2012) provide a Nordic perspective on the global challenge faced by public libraries to redefine their space so as to accommodate both the physical and the virtual aspects of the library. They envision a library that offers four overlapping spaces that can be used either physically or virtually. Their model includes space for inspiration, space for learning, space for meeting and performative/creative space.

As public libraries in the USA grapple with the challenges confronting them, they are finding it difficult to give up or eliminate any of the activities they currently perform. A publication from the American Library Association (ALA) (Levien, 2011) identifies some 14 functions of public libraries, all of which have been the purview of public libraries for years; there is nothing new or unusual about any of them. What is (and will continue to be) new is how public libraries are offering these functions to their communities. The report also identifies that the public library faces competition in providing each function. While the idea of competition is not new, the reality of that competition needs to be recognized more openly and seen as the challenge that it is.

Academic libraries find themselves facing a number of challenges in the second decade of the 21st century. Some of these sound very familiar: concerns about space, about collections and services, about technology, and more. Three challenges identified for academic libraries and their staffs (but impacting on other information environments as well) are: (1) a shift from being an information worker to an information creator; (2) a shift from addressing the general information needs of their customers to providing more customized, individual-oriented information; and (3) a shift from collection management to knowledge management (Thomas, Satpathi and Satpathi, 2010). The general thrust of Thomas et al.'s article is how various professional associations have been helping information professionals to update their knowledge and skills so as to address these and other challenges since the mid-1990s. They review a variety of continuing education opportunities offered by the ALA, IFLA, the Chartered Institute of Library and Information Professions and, in their own country, the Indian Association of Special Libraries and Information Centers. The authors find that continuing education opportunities offered by North American and European library associations are more diverse in nature and more available than those offered elsewhere (like in India). The programmes and workshops identified focus on a number of management-related topics, as well as on technology.

Libraries respond in various ways to the challenges they face. One of the more dramatic/overarching responses is to reorganize (or realign, to use a more contemporary term) the library. An analysis of which units were dropped, which units were revised/merged/moved and which units were added in a realignment provides graphic evidence of how the reorganized library reflects the new priorities for its services and content. The Oregon State University (OSU) libraries provide a example of this in a realignment that was implemented in 2010 (Nutefall and Chadwell, 2012). While a comparison of the before-and-after organizational charts doesn't appear to be that startling, a look at what the realigned sub-units will do (or no longer do) begins to get one's attention, as subject specialists, cataloguing and journal claiming are all identified as functions that can be left behind as the OSU libraries move forward.

Management fads and fashions

What we can see from the challenges mentioned above, as well as others you may know about, is that libraries of all types face many of the same issues that confront any organization today and will do in the immediate future. While most libraries do not measure their success in strict financial terms of profit and loss, they still need to focus their attention and energy on the same issues as other organizations (both for-profit and not-for-profit) do, such as budgets, personnel, customer satisfaction, space, technology and the like; basic management concerns for the successful operation of any organization. Although the LIS field has specialized journals, workshops and conferences dealing with library management, for the most part we have adapted our models, paradigms and theories (or whatever term you prefer) of library management from the larger management arena in which we all live and work. There are few, if any, models of management that originated in a library. And this is not a negative aspect that we necessarily need to change. Most management ideas are general in nature and can be applied in numerous environments. Thus, when we come across models aimed at helping to make our employees more productive, our customers more satisfied and our finances more positive and stable, we have a tendency to be interested. The good news is that there is no shortage of these ideas in the general management literature; the bad news, likewise, is that there is no shortage of these ideas in the general management literature.

Management as a profession, and certainly as a topic that can be taught and studied, is relatively new, and younger than librarianship in that regard. Some view the management field as having started with Henri Fayol in Europe toward the end of the 19th century, and with Frederick Taylor in the USA in the early 20th century. For others, management did not emerge as a profession until the end of World War 2 and the post-war era of recovery, expansion and globalization. Trying to pinpoint an exact starting date for the profession of management (as the LIS field in the USA has done, with 1876 and the start of the ALA) would be somewhat arbitrary and not particularly useful. A review of the literature reveals that many of these management models/theories dating back to the 1950s have been introduced, adopted with a varying amount of success and then discontinued or abandoned. This cycle of introduction, adoption and abandonment has led those in the field of management to refer to such models as management fads or fashions. Over the years, some of these fads and fashions have made their way into our libraries, both in the form of resources that discuss these fads (and so they are on our shelves and in our databases) and in the form of techniques/ approaches that we use to manage our organizations (and so they impact on the people who work in them and the people who use them). We need to explore the extent to which any of these fads can help us to meet the challenges we are facing.

Defining fads and fashions

The first thing we need to do is define what is meant by a management fad or fashion. Some authors have made a distinction between the two, while others use these terms somewhat interchangeably. (In my research for this article I came across as many sources using the term 'fad' as using the term 'fashion', plus others using yet other terms.) The person most responsible for studying management fads and fashions is Eric Abrahamson, who first looked at the topic in his PhD dissertation of 1989 and published his first article on the topic in 1991. While both of these works use 'fads and fashions' in their titles, by 1996, as Abrahamson continued to do research on the subject, he seemed to settle on the term 'management fashions', which he defined as 'transitory collective beliefs that certain management techniques are at the forefront of management progress' (Abrahamson, 1996, 254). We can compare that with the following comprehensive definition of management fads: 'managerial interventions which appear to be innovative, rational, and functional and are aimed at encouraging better organizational performance' (Carson et al., 1999). (It is interesting to note that essentially this same group of authors, in a work published the following year, used the term fashion rather than fad.) Both of these definitions clearly see fads or fashions as something positive (i.e. 'forefront of management progress' and 'encouraging better organizational performance'), but at the same time they hedge their bets in that regard (i.e. 'transitory beliefs' and 'which appear to be'). So, there may be more to a management fad/fashion than initially meets the eye.

Labelling something as a 'fad' is typically considered negative, which may be one reason why some authors prefer the term 'fashion', to avoid the reader's prejudging the value of a management idea. Despite this, the past labelling of management techniques as fads has not prevented other fads from being introduced. Of course, those introducing the next fad-to-be don't see their idea from that perspective (although no doubt they would prefer their idea to be labelled a fashion); so why would they hesitate to share their ideas with the world? Certain conditions also need to be present for any organization to consider trying the most recent fashion when it is introduced.

Adopting new fads or fashions

Three possible conditions stand out as factors that would assist in the adoption of new management ideas. First, there are environmental pressures that impact on the organization on a regular basis. If conditions are relatively stable and the status quo appears to be working, there is little reason to consider change. However, when conditions are turbulent, when we're faced with increased competition and future funding uncertainty (among other factors), we become more receptive to trying new things.

Second, there are certain organizational characteristics that assist in fad adoption. We are continually told that to be a leading/smart/excellent/ your-favourite-descriptor-here organization, we need to be willing to accept some degree of risk and try new/different things. So, if we want to be viewed in this way by our peers, we are a bit more susceptible to becoming an 'early adopter'.

Third, once a few organizations get things going, touting some new management idea, the 'bandwagon' effect kicks in and the need to conform to prevailing trends helps the new ideas to spread. We may not want to be the organization that takes the horses from the stable, hitches them up to the bandwagon and takes the reins; but we also don't want to be the organization that is running to catch up, barely hanging on to the bandwagon, with our feet dragging in the dirt.

There is an additional factor that we also need to consider: what if this new management concept actually works? The concepts/techniques that we now recognize as management fads/fashions all started with claims of dramatic improvement in some organization's performance, productivity, quality, customer satisfaction and more. There is never any doubt (at least on the part of those who developed the idea) that the method/mind-set proposed won't work for any organization under any circumstances. And I doubt that any organization feels that it performs so well that there is no room for improvement or that it has no worry about competitors. Miller, Hartwick and Le Breton-Miller identified eight characteristics of management fads/fashions that make them appear attractive and worthwhile:

Simple/straightforward – A fad's ideas are easy to communicate, comprehend, and reduce to a small number of factors, dimensions, or characteristics. Clear-cut distinctions, perfect contrasts, and ideal types are proposed. Simple solutions are suggested.

Promising results – Fad auteurs are confidently didactic. There is no false humility or hedging. Fads promise results such as greater control and efficiency, more motivated and productive workers, more satisfied customers, or some other valued result.

Universal – Fads propose solutions for everyone. Imparted truths are said to apply to almost all organizations, functions, tasks, individuals, or cultures. Fads claim enormous generality and universal relevance.

Step-down capability – Fads have the capacity to be implemented in ritualistic and superficial ways. Recommendations can be implemented quickly and easily, often without having much effect on organizational practices. Recommendations involving large expenditures of resources or substantial redistributions of power can be avoided.

In tune with zeitgeist – Fads resonate with the major trends or business problems of the day. They respond to challenges that are broadly felt and openly discussed. These might result from deficiencies in current administrative practices, technology changes, or shifts in economic or social conditions. Solutions are in tune with prevailing values.

Novel, not radical – Fads are novel, not radical. They question existing assumptions, criticize widespread practices, and point to fresh ways of doing things. However, this novelty is not so much a new discovery as a rediscovery and repackaging of older ideas, values, and approaches.

Legitimacy via gurus and star examples – Fads are supported by tales of excellent companies and the status and prestige of gurus, not by solid empirical evidence. Stories of corporate heroes and organizational successes provide role models and suggest prestigious adherents, lending an aura of legitimacy to the ideas being espoused.

Lively, entertaining – Fads are almost always presented in a way that can be described as concrete, articulate, bold, memorable and upbeat. They are filled with labels and buzzwords, lists and acronyms. Interesting anecdotes and corporate war stories abound. Descriptions are vivid and extreme, making fads fun to read about and listen to.

(Miller, Hartwick and Le Breton-Miller, 2004, 11)

The challenge, of course, is to see all or most of these characteristics as the new concept is introduced, although by definition a fad/fashion is identified as such in hindsight, when the promises made are not realized, except perhaps by a few organizations (star examples) because certain conditions existed for those organizations at a specific time. One of the best examples of this that we have is the firms recognized in 1982 as 'excellent' by Tom Peters and Robert Waterman. For better or worse, they became the focus of management authors and researchers, and in less than a decade over half of them had experienced set-backs that negated their excellence as initially defined by Peters and Waterman (Miller, 1990).

Library fads and fashions

The LIS community should be aware of the continuous cycle of management fads/fashions for at least two reasons. First, we have not been immune to adopting various fads over the years in an effort to be more effective and efficient. This is not a bad thing; as we have seen, fads typically show promise when they are introduced and it is not until a few years later that we begin to recognize the limitations of these models for managing our organizations. As the challenges we confront dictate that changes are needed, we would not be fulfilling our managerial responsibilities if we dismissed any new management idea out of hand. And sometimes the decision to adopt what turns out to be a passing fad or fashion may not be ours to make. I remember that during my first professional position in an academic library we adopted what was called 'participatory management'. I knew this because I read the memo from our library director informing all of us that, as of a specific date, we'd be a participatory management shop. And the only reason why he wrote that memo was because the university's president had made a similar announcement to his executive committee and council of deans. Our president had recently returned from attending some conference where the 'wonders' of participatory management had been successfully (at least to him) presented. (Which leads me to suggest that university administrators should never be allowed off campus, except for sporting events and fund raising – but that's another chapter for a different book.)

The second reason why we need to be aware of management fashions is that we often contribute to them by legitimizing these ideas through having the books (and now other media) that espouse them in our collections. Again, because these fashions are introduced with such promise, and often from well-established authors, one could easily make a case that we'd be remiss in not adding these works to our collections. Since the mid-1990s, however, a few things have come to light that might create a bit of doubt. In 1995, *Business Week* reported on a fairly elaborate scheme to 'game the system' and ensure that the book *The Discipline of Market Leaders* made it onto the *New York Times'* best-seller list and remained there for some time – one of the hallmarks of getting one's management ideas diffused widely and a necessary prerequisite to attaining fad/fashion status (Stern, 1995). A few years later, Stuart Crainer (1998) reported that a number of high-profile, best-selling management books had been ghost written, with the named authors having little or nothing to do with the actual content of the works. Finally, at the end of 2001 Tom Peters revealed in an interview that some of the data that he and co-author Robert Waterman had presented in *In Search of Excellence* was not real. Any library that purchased any of these works had no doubt acted in good faith in making those acquisitions, so it is hard to be overly critical. Furthermore, similar allegations have been made against other books by other authors in other fields. It may not be a question of not acquiring such material, but more a question of what we do when these revelations come to light. This is an intriguing question, but one more appropriate for a volume on collection management, not organizational management, so we'll press on.

Fads and fashions in changing times

What does all this mean for the LIS community? What assistance is available for those charged with managing our libraries and information centres (large, small or in between)? As the title of this book suggests, libraries (as well as other organizations) find themselves dealing with disruption and uncertainty, two conditions that rarely enhance productivity or progress. As we grapple with the world today, we need to remember two factors: (1) our libraries are constantly changing and (2) no two libraries are alike. Neither of these is particularly startling, but each seems to be regularly overlooked. First, regardless of what may appear to be occurring, every organization is in constant flux. The same group of people could work at the same jobs in the same location for years and change would still occur. Our clientele will change, our collections and services will change and how we do those 'same jobs' will change, because of technology and other factors. Additionally, each of us is changing: we are not the same person that we were yesterday or will be tomorrow. What we experience today gets added to our individual 'database' of total experience and alters our perspective. As we (as well as those around us) get a day closer to retirement our outlook on work and our motivation for being there changes. Since any organization is made up of individuals, as those individuals change, so too does the organization.

Second, no two libraries are alike. While many libraries may be similar in a number of ways, essentially they are all different. Their staffs are different, their clienteles are different, the environments in which they operate are different. Thus, what works for one library may not work for another, regardless of the similarities between them. Programmes, services, collections and the like that are well received at one library could be a complete failure at another.

When we think about what a new management concept represents, we also need to remember these two factors, so that we can analyse/interpret the new management concept from an informed perspective. As we've seen, many of these management ideas end up being described as a 'fad' or a 'fashion', and both terms are used in a less than complimentary manner. However, the fashion analogy may hold some promise if we extend it beyond the fairly superficial use to which it has typically been put. Fads are by definition temporary, and many fashions are in fact fads because they are introduced, spread quickly and then peter out, only to be found in consignment or second-hand stores. On the other hand, some fashions are more lasting and provide a 'classic' look that we can wear for years. And, I suspect that most of our closets have garments that fit into both categories. The management models that eventually attained 'fashion/fad' status all started out well intended, usually with examples of how well they worked for a handful of organizations; so that's what gets presented to us – that one successful model as *the* way to do things. And this is fine if our organization resembles the organization(s) used to create the model. Of course, even if there is a match today, will the resemblance be as strong tomorrow? After all, any garment is going to look good on the model as they come down the catwalk to show off the 'fashion' for the first time – that's what it is designed to do. But while we're 'oohing' and 'aahing' over the model before us, we should be asking ourselves how this particular garment will fit in with the rest of our current wardrobe and what it will look like hanging in the closet.

Maybe instead of focusing on the model, we should be looking at the pattern and the fundamental design of the garment. As anyone who has made or altered a garment knows, the pattern is the foundation upon which it is based. The pattern gives us an idea of what the garment will look like and hence what it may be used for – regardless of the fabric used to construct the garment, the colour of the fabric, the stitching used to hold it together and more. Of course many garments are designed with specific fabrics, colours and stitching in mind, but working from the pattern level, customization is definitely possible. Additionally, most commercial patterns can accommodate garments of different sizes and include provision for the garment to be altered over time, recognizing that the same person, just like the same organization, will change and alterations will be necessary to extend the garment's usefulness/ wearability.

As we make decisions about the type or 'style' of management to use within our organizations, we can take a few cues from the decisions we make about the style we hope to project through the garments we choose to wear each day. We can try to be very fashionable, seeking out new styles and being among the first to be seen in a particular garment. Or we can focus our sense of fashion around a few styles that we know and add elements of new or changing styles as they fit in and enhance our current wardrobe.

Just as we individually stand before our closets, deciding what to wear to work today and (hopefully) ask ourselves 'What do I hope to accomplish today, with whom will I interact today, what image do I want to project today, and how will this garment or combination of garments help me to do that?' so our organizations should ask similar questions; questions about the way they will be structured, the way power and influence will be dispersed, the way decisions will be made, the way resources will be allocated and more should help our organizations to identify the appropriate pattern of management to use and when that pattern may need to be altered so as to accommodate changes that the organization needs to address.

Conclusion

A consistent theme among those studying management fads/fashions explains that managers find these fads attractive because they don't have to study their own organizations as closely or think about ways to improve things when they adopt 'off the shelf' solutions. The other side of the equation tells us that 'management is the art of thinking about systems as a whole, and uses discipline to identify the pieces and their relationships. It is about creating an entity with value in a marketplace, and instilling in everyone within an organization a sense of purpose relative to that value-adding entity and a set of activities' (Shelley, 1996, 13). In other words, management is work; worse yet, management is hard work. Those looking to avoid that level of effort rarely succeed. For the most part, libraries have done a reasonably good job of not getting caught up in looking for an 'off the shelf' approach to management. But as the pace of change accelerates, competition increases and the challenges facing any organization become more similar, library managers at all levels need to rededicate themselves to the management work ahead.

References

Abrahamson, E. (1989) Fads and Fashions in Administrative Technologies, unpublished doctoral dissertation, New York University.

Abrahamson, E. (1991) Managerial Fads and Fashions: the diffusion and rejection of innovations, *Academy of Management Review*, **16** (3), 586–612.

Abrahamson, E. (1996) Management Fashion, *Academy of Management Review*, **21** (1), 254–85.

Adeyoyin, S. O., Imam, A. and Bello, T. O. (2012) Management of Change in the 21st Century Libraries and Information Centres [electronic version], *Library Philosophy and Practice*, Paper 695, http://digitalcommons.unl.edu/libphil/prac/695.

Carson, P. P., Lanier, P. A., Carson, K. D. and Brikenmeier, B. J. (1999) A Historical Perspective on Fad Adoption and Abandonment, *Journal of Management History*, **5** (6), 320–33.

Crainer, S. (1998) In Search of the Real Author, *Management Today*, May, 50–4.

Frey, T. (2009) *Future Libraries: once a refuge, now they mean business*, www.futuristspeaker.com/2009/04/future-libraries-once-a-refuge-now-they-mean-business.

Jochumsen, H., Rasmussen, C. H. and Skot-Hansen, D. (2012) The Four Spaces – a new model for the public library, *New Library World*, **113** (11/12), 586–97.

Law, D. (2011) As for the Future, Your Task Is not to Foresee It, but to Enable It, *IFLA Journal*, **37** (4), 269–75.

Levien, R. E. (2011) *Confronting the Future – strategic visions for the 21st century public library*, Policy Brief No. 4, June, ALA Office for Information Technology Policy, www.ala.org/offices/sites/ala.org.offices/files/content/oitp/publications/policybriefs/confronting_the_futu.pdf.

Miller, D. (1990) *The Icarus Paradox*, HarperBusiness.

Miller, D., Hartwick, J. and Le Breton-Miller, I. (2004) How to Detect a Management Fad – and Distinguish It from a Classic, *Business Horizons*, **47** (4), 7–16.

Nutefall, J. E. and Chadwell, F. A. (2012) Preparing for the 21st Century: academic library realignment, *New Library World*, **113** (3/4), 162–73.

Peters, T. (2001) Tom Peter's True Confessions, *Fast Company*, **53** (December), 80–92.

Shelley, G. C. (1996) The Search for the Universal Management Elixir, *Business Quarterly*, **60** (4), 11–13.

Stern, W. (1995) Did Dirty Tricks Create a Best-seller? *Business Week*, (7 August), **3436**, 22.

Thomas, V. T., Satpathi, C. and Satpathi, J. N. (2010) Emerging Challenges in Academic Librarianship and Role of Library Associations in Professional Updating, *Library Management*, **31** (8/9), 594–609.

CHAPTER 3

The Five Rules of Engagement for librarians: aux Ranganathan's laws of library science

Choy Fatt Cheong

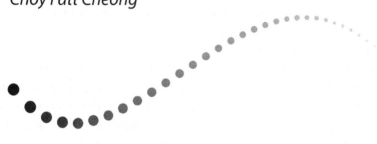

Introduction

There is no doubt that librarians have crossed the threshold of a new era in the history of their profession since the advent of the internet. Global connectivity has brought information and people together instantly and seamlessly, which seems to suggest less need for mediation, co-ordination and facilitation by libraries. Yet, the information landscape has become more complex, which may create new demands that libraries and librarians can fulfil. Librarians are adapting to meet new needs, doing and planning work that was inconceivable in the past. As technology advances, librarians will move further away from old concerns. However, we should remain tethered to the core ideals of the library as an institution that promotes the use of information to deepen people's knowledge and understanding of the world. To do this, we need to be constantly reminded of the impact of our role in achieving this ideal, regardless of the future functions we perform. This paper proposes a practical way to do this.

Focusing on users

Throughout history, libraries have performed their role in a variety of ways, adapting to the needs of the people they serve and using the technology of the day. In the past, libraries focused on providing and organizing scarce information resources for use. They also took on the role of preserving the intellectual work of the past and present by building and maintaining collections. Today libraries collect, own and disseminate information resources in a less intensive way, because of changes in communication technology and publishing practices. The new, complex information environment, characterized by information abundance, ease of accessibility and disruptive interactions, has moved libraries away from collecting and towards playing a greater role in facilitating people's more effective use of information.

Users have always been an important component of the library mission, although they have occupied different degrees of prominence in different eras. Users will be the key to our profession, as collection was before circa 1990. Our impact on users depends on our interaction with them, in face-to-face or in virtual modes. Whether or not libraries will be useful and valued by users depends on the relationship between librarians and users. The mere provision of access to resources will not be sufficient reason for high investment in libraries by stakeholders. As people strive to make sense of the complex information environment, there is a greater potential for the expertise and services provided by librarians to contribute significantly to the value of libraries.

Even as information activities become increasingly mediated by intelligent systems and technologies, it is hard to imagine, nor do most of us wish for, a scenario where machines communicate and do all the thinking, learning and discovery work for us. Machines can aid and extend our powers, as they have done in the past, but human inputs and relationships, at least in intellectual activities, will always be necessary if we are not to live in a dysfunctional world. This is the basic premise of this discussion on the importance of librarians' continuing their effort to engage with users.

Ranganathan's Five Laws of Library Science

In 1931 the well-known Indian librarian S. R. Ranganathan bequeathed to the library world his Five Laws of Library Science, namely (1) books are for use, (2) every reader his [her] book, (3) every book its reader, (4) save the time of the reader and (5) the library is a growing organism (Ranganathan, 1931). Although the Five Laws have been around for more than 80 years, the spirit and intent behind them remain highly relevant and inspirational. The term 'books' in our current context is just a metaphor for any knowledge expressed in recorded information. The Five Laws urge libraries to be totally focused on enabling people through knowledge. They recognize the diversity of interests among people and the importance of catering for them. They place the reader or user at the centre of libraries and recognize that they are the key to all successful libraries. Librarians thus serve users or people who are seeking knowledge with which to empower themselves. This user-centric view is more important than ever before, in this era of the democratization of knowledge.

The Five Rules of Engagement for librarians

Inspired by Ranganathan's Five Laws of Library Science, I would like to propose 'Five Rules of Engagement' for librarians. The purpose is to provide a guide to how we should approach our work as librarians from a user-centric perspective, in particular, its focus on cultivating, sustaining and advancing our engagement and relationship with users. Devoting more effort to user engagement is a natural development as we shift our focus from collections to users. Furthermore, as we cater for the new needs of users, our profession will be more diverse in the range of work that it does. As we depend increasingly on technological solutions and intelligent screen interfaces there is a danger that we might forget the real, blood-and-flesh user, the fulfilment of whose needs is the ultimate aim of our work. The antidote must be greater user engagement. As more librarians become involved with user activities it is useful for a library to establish and promote a common credo of service so as to ensure a consistent approach to user-centred work. The Five Rules (or goals) aux Ranganathan's famous Five Laws provide a useful device to communicate the stance and approach of library service.

First rule: librarians are experts

The value of a librarian, or indeed any professional, lies in the difference in knowledge, skills and ability between the professional and lay person (or user) in some sphere of activity in which the latter needs assistance. If users have the same knowledge and skills as a librarian, there is no reason why they need the librarian. Therefore librarians must be experts in some domain that enables them to solve some sets of real-world problems that others are not able to resolve or to resolve efficiently. Just as we seek out experts to help with our own problems such as an illness, a building defect or a psychological condition, others will seek us out only if we are able to provide expertise to resolve their information problems better than they can. By expertise we mean the combination of knowledge, skills and abilities that enables an expert to provide added value to others.

There are many attempts in the literature to describe the expertise that librarians possess or should possess and this discussion does not intend to summarize or review these. Suffice it to say that the expertise required of librarians varies with time, particularly now that we are living in an age of disruptive changes. The changes are particularly drastic for librarians, as we are very much at the centre of the ongoing information revolution where, among other things, users are more empowered in carrying out their information activities. In the eyes of many information seekers, libraries today form just a small part of the vast information landscape. Yet, the new information environment has also brought new issues and challenges for many users. Making sense of information and using it effectively is getting more difficult for users. The expertise of librarians, gained from knowledge, practice and experience of users' information-seeking behaviour, the characteristics of information and the information industry, fits in with this new need to a T. However, unlike in the past, our expertise must be concerned with the entire information universe and not just the library world. For example, we need to have expert understanding of the nature and use of the variety of information in the internet and not just the well-structured sources from the world of print publishing.

One of the strengths of librarians is their focus on users' needs. Apart from having a greater familiarity with and grasp of information issues, librarians are also known for their user-centred approach. As a case in point, the traditional reference interview techniques focus on getting users to discover their real information needs through a series of open questions, rather than just providing 'expert' answers immediately. In the era of the self-empowered individual, it is more crucial for librarians to have strong skills in facilitation, rather than to rely purely on specialized knowledge. In a sense, it requires librarians to shed their 'expertness' in order to help people along, as noted by Stover (2004): 'The postmodern librarian will recognize that professional resources and professional knowledge are not secret commodities to be protected or monopolized. Instead, this librarian will seek to share these gifts with patrons in a relational, interdependent, and non-hierarchical manner.' This ability to guide and work with others so as to let them find solutions to their problems and achieve their goals in learning and research is a valuable form of expertise.

Librarians as experts have the advantage of being able to use the library as an institution to add value to their work, even as they look beyond the library world. It has often been argued that librarians should be untethered from libraries, as they can offer expertise independently of libraries. However, libraries are necessary to strengthen the work of librarians. It might be useful to see the role of librarians as being in two areas, the one in managing a library to provide resources and services and the other in providing advice and expertise on information-related issues. Although the two are not mutually exclusive, this approach could help us to clarify the administrative and the professional aspects of our work. As administrators we focus on managing a library as an effective entity so as to provide useful services to groups of people or to society at large. As professionals, we rely on a unique body of knowledge and accumulated practical experience to add value for a client or user. It is this latter role that defines and characterizes our work. Librarians should be primarily tied to their body of professional knowledge. Libraries are the vehicles in which we operate; they provide the tools, infrastructure and support system for librarians to provide expertise to others.

Second rule: every librarian is a friend of users

Friends are people whom we can trust and rely on for help, and vice versa. We should treat our users like we treat our friends, i.e. always having their best interest at heart. Like friends, they will do the same for us when needed. Here, we speak of friendship as an attitude rather than as a personal state such as finding solace and comfort in a close relationship. Obviously we are limited by the Dunbar number (Dunbar, 1992), which states that there is a limit (about 150) to the number of stable relationships we can sustain. Unless we work in a small community, for example, in a special library, the idea of being a friend to users refers more to an approach and our disposition in working with users. Building good working relationships with others is essential in any work environment, but for librarians this is critical.

Perhaps another way to express this is as having empathy with users. Users who seek help from librarians are as varied as the books on the shelves. There is no standard answer to a query. Each user comes with a different state of knowledge and disposition and should be treated in accordance with their needs. Some may need more hand holding than others for a similar request; for example, guidance in doing literature reviews. A good librarian will adjust their approach and put themselves in the same frame of mind as a user who comes for help. A friend who willingly helps will be patient, supportive, understanding, eager to please and not condescending. If we treat each user the same way as we treat our friends, our effectiveness will be much greater.

One of the hallmarks of any friend is their willingness to share, and there is a lot that a librarian can share with their users, whether they be students, teachers or researchers. Obviously, our knowledge of the information world such as books, journals, e-resources, publishers and the publishing trade is of interest to our users, since these are connected to their work activities. The ground of common interest can help in initiating and building friendly relationships that are mutually beneficial and satisfying. Librarians are also connected to a wide range of users. As interested by-standers in relationships between different classes of users, i.e. between students and teachers, administrators and researchers, researchers and students etc., librarians have a non-partisan, useful and interesting perspective on the community they work in.

Being a friend to users is not limited to one-to-one transactions but also applies to an overall consideration of users in all areas of library work. When we are planning new services or initiating changes we should ask ourselves how they will affect our friends, the users. When we deal with our friends we treat them as individuals and not as numbers or an abstract quantity. In fact, the mere act of replacing the word 'user' with 'friend' might cause a minor shift in our thinking and our approach to offering library services.

The benefits of treating users as friends are obvious. It will help to remove barriers of communication and allow us to do our work better. There will be greater user satisfaction and it will most certainly lead to repeat visits and calls for assistance. Overall, it will increase the usefulness and value of libraries and librarians.

Third rule: every encounter with users should add value for them

Librarianship is essentially a service-oriented profession. We provide our key services through encounters with our users – whether this be face to face, over the phone, via e-mail or through social media. For the user, the purpose of the encounter is to obtain something they do not have, to resolve a problem or to increase their understanding of some issue. For the encounter to be successful, a positive change must take place for the user and value must be added by the librarian. For example, when a user approaches a reading-advisory librarian for guidance on interesting books to read in a particular genre, the librarian provides added value through their recommendation and the user goes away with a positive outcome.

Not all encounters will result in a clear, positive outcome for users, for many reasons. For example, a library may not have the required resources to satisfy the user, or the request may be out of the range of services provided by the library. A good librarian will not stop at this and allow the encounter to remain unproductive but will instead find other ways to add value. In the first example, the librarian could suggest close alternatives, and in the second they might perhaps refer the user to other service points or to organizations that can provide the required service. In both instances, value has been created even though the librarian may not have completely resolved the problem. Furthermore, when we have to resort to alternatives, this often gives us an opportunity to be creative and resourceful. These opportunities allow us to grow and develop professionally as individuals. They might also lead us to create new services when we detect a pattern of needs from these service failures.

Even in situations when we are unable to satisfy a user request or offer alternatives, the librarian needs to create opportunities for future encounters. Users should go away from such encounters with the feeling that the failure to obtain what they need is due not to the incompetence of the librarian or the poor services of the library but to the specificity of their request. They must be made to feel confident that the present failure to meet their needs is not indicative of the future success rate of their requests for assistance. This feeling could be influenced by the demeanour of the librarian and the user's impression of the library. Sometimes all it takes is a smile and a genuine desire to please.

In a typical commercial transaction, the sales person wants to give the customer something of value in exchange for profit for the shop. The librarian does not charge users (not directly, anyway), so what do we want to get in return? In the long run, it is continuing patronage of our service, but the noblest reason is of course to do good and to have the satisfaction of making a difference in people's intellectual development and understanding of the world. This is one of the great distinguishing differences between librarians and commercial entities, and should be emphasized often. In this way we build a store of good will and trust of real value both for the library and for society in general.

Fourth rule: users must have high demand and expectation of librarians

Most people, even regular library users, think of librarians as administrators of books and library collections for lending. It is quite common to encounter users who are surprised even by the routine range of services performed by librarians, such as teaching information literacy skills, setting up digital repositories, providing readers' advisory services, guiding students in literature reviews etc. This is an indication of the low expectations most people have of librarians.

We will be doomed if users continue to think of libraries as just a place to borrow books, study in quiet corners and nap in between classes, and expect nothing more. When people have low expectations of a service they will value it less or neglect it completely. It is particularly dangerous for us if people associate librarians' roles with areas that are seen to be being side-lined because of new technology. This will lead to the erosion of our economic value, even though we may have moved on to higher-value work.

On the other hand, when people expect more from us this shows that they recognize we can deliver a service that they need. If we shy away in fear of being inundated with too much work or if we lack the confidence to enter into new territories, then people will look to alternatives. We will be left behind with existing and 'safe' roles, but they may not last us long. Similarly, librarians should welcome criticism, as it is an indication that we can do better and have higher potential value. If nobody criticizes what we do, it means that no one really cares about what we do.

In fact, we should be more proactive. We should actively generate demand for our services. Just like any thriving business we need to be aggressive in seeking out opportunities to do more work and to expand our field of operation and influence. For profit-making companies it is natural and essential to chase after business. In libraries and other cost-centre operations there is always a tendency to conserve resources and be cautious about over-extending themselves. However, if we are too cautious, in the end we will have no valuable services to offer. There will be no compelling reasons for our parent bodies to continue to commit resources for us to exist. To succeed, we must make sure that people continue to depend on us to meet their needs.

Fifth rule: the library's critical role in knowledge work must be widely recognized and acknowledged

People from all levels of society, from young to old, poor to rich and uneducated to educated, have no problems in identifying the roles of popular professions such as medicine, law, accountancy and architecture. They know who to go to when they are sick, have disputes with others, need to sort out business problems or build their homes. For these professions, their purpose and function in society is deeply entrenched and well established. The library profession is not entirely unknown to the public. On the contrary, it is quite well known, but it is based on a narrow spectrum of activities (e.g. as lenders of books) and not associated with the full range of work that professional librarians normally do.

There is a higher purpose in librarianship that is not often articulated and recognized. Other professions mentioned in the examples have the advantage of dealing with basic life issues such as health and illness, disputes, business and shelter, while the higher goals of librarianship are not clearly connected to the activities popularly associated with our work. For librarians to play an effective role, they need to articulate the higher goals of their work clearly, so that the public, employers and other institutions are aware of these. This will lead to more opportunities for our profession to contribute its best to society.

What is this higher goal? The work of libraries is very intimately connected to the advancement of human knowledge. Since recorded history, libraries have played critical roles in the preservation and transmission of mankind's knowledge, albeit silently. Libraries provide the platform for those giants on whose metaphorical shoulders Newton stood, as he famously remarked about the importance of previously accumulated knowledge in the advancement of knowledge. The idea of a 'library' as an accumulation of knowledge on which to draw is a powerful metaphor used in all areas of work. We need to define the purpose of libraries in terms of a greater outcome:

> Libraries collectively are the main instrument that preserve and transmit
> this body of accumulated knowledge or 'knowledge base' ... Libraries provide
> information within an appropriate context to help transform information into
> knowledge in an individual's mind. A library, as a whole, is a knowledge base
> and not just a mere collection of information resources or materials. Just as a
> database is more than a collection of documents and texts (it has search and
> collation powers), a knowledge base would include all the structural,
> organizational and contextual elements that help individuals turn
> information into their private knowledge.
>
> (Choy, 2007)

Seen from this greater perspective, the library is a powerful institution
that has a great, positive impact on the development of individuals and
society. Much of the work that librarians do can be couched in terms of
higher goals. Reframing our work in the greater context also allows us to
explore new areas of work so as to further the goals of our profession. It is
important for librarians to continuously advocate and promote their roles
so that they may continue to contribute to the rich intellectual heritage of
humankind.

Management use of the Five Rules

The Five Rules introduced above are an expression of the user-centred
philosophy of libraries and, in particular, the stance that librarians take
in engaging with users. This philosophy is based on the premise that the
actual relationship and engagement with users matters, not just good
design of systems and services using user-centred principles. It does not
matter whether engagement with users is in face-to-face mode or in
virtual space, so long as a personal link is established between the
librarian and the user.

The Five Rules can be viewed as a useful aphorism for aligning our daily
practice with our philosophical belief. The advantage of expressing the
user-centred approach in short, succinct and aphoristic statements rather
than in a long treatise is that it is a better way of drawing the
practitioner's attention to what is essentially a very practical matter. The
success and widespread influence of Ranganathan's Five Laws of Library

Science is due to not just their brilliant content but also to the way in which the philosophy is expressed in their pithy form.

Librarians are the key to delivering user-centred services and interaction with users. Library managers must therefore ensure that their librarian staff apply a consistent approach in engaging with users that is in line with their user-centric philosophy. They could use the Five Rules as a framework for the following:

- discussion with staff members on common values to adhere to
- constructing an inventory of current practices to align the library to a user-centred approach
- training tools for new staff to introduce staff members to a user-centred philosophy.

Although many librarians may profess themselves to be user centred, when it comes to engagement with their users it cannot be assumed that everyone understands or agrees on what this really means. Dedicated and open discussion among staff members on each of the Five Rules can provide an important opportunity to examine the core beliefs of a library and its staff. Discussion of the Five Rules can trigger staff members to recall real-life examples from their daily practice and use them to affirm, vary or even disagree with these rules. The Five Rules are not meant to be a definitive and uniform prescription for user-centric engagement with users in all libraries, but rather a starting point for a library to build consensus relevant to its circumstances. The process of discussion using the Five Rules framework will help to clarify and reinforce user-centred practices in a library.

It is also useful for a library to take stock of its current library services, policies and practices and to test if they conform to the expectation of engagement with users. For example, building staff expertise is not often thought of as part of user-centred services. If we think of adding value to the work and development of users as a key goal, then we need to identify how we can make a difference for users and what expertise our staff need in order to enable this. This might lead to adjustment in staff development plans and other library policy changes. Similarly, for Rule 5, a library might want to assess whether the roles of its librarians and the services they offer are recognized in the community. Are there indicators that point to this and, if not, could they be introduced or created? More importantly, if anecdotal evidence points to doubts on this score, efforts could be initiated to raise this awareness.

The Five Rules also provide a good framework for developing a more interactive induction and organizational socialization programme for new staff. Training and induction of new staff are important in ensuring continuity of organizational culture and practice, thus helping to maintain the identity, character and values of an organization. Such programmes help new staff to integrate successfully into their new workplace so that they can quickly become effective members of the team. However, this is largely a one-way process, i.e. from the organization to the individual. As pointed out by Antonacopoulou and Guttel (2010), 'the main objective of institutionalized staff induction programs is the newcomer's adjustment to organizational needs. Consequently, institutionalized induction programs raise adjustment pressure and reduce the options for newcomers to innovate and to change existing expectations' (p. 40). In growing, dynamic organizations in an environment of rapid change it is important to have a mechanism whereby fresh input into the core ideals and values of an organization can be debated, tested, reviewed and possibly revised. 'A practice perspective embraces tensions as a natural part of the way organizations emerge hence, acknowledges the positive role of conflict between newcomers and incumbents, where inductees have the potential to shake existing norms and value sets, as much as they are being taught how to reproduce these' (Antonacopoulou and Guttel, 2010, 43). Ideas from new staff, untainted by organizational indoctrination, could be a useful source of input to this approach. The Five Rules could act as a framework to build this process, as it is a set of general aspirations of the profession that address the core concerns of a library without being too specific to an organization and possibly holding back free discussion by newcomers.

Conclusion

Many would agree that librarianship is today undergoing profound changes that by definition will significantly change the character of libraries and the work of librarians. Nevertheless, certain fundamentals are unlikely to change. One of these is the user-centric approach to the librarian's work. Whatever changes occur, our work is driven by the needs of users. They are the keystone of our profession. Librarians are the primary agents in engaging with users and their failure or success in doing so will shape the future of the profession. Whatever form that user engagement takes, it must be based on a mutually beneficial relationship between the librarian and the user. The onus is on the librarian to maintain, develop and advance this relationship, as users can seek alternatives, no matter how inadequate or ineffective they are from our perspective. The proposed Five Rules of Engagement are a constant reminder to the practising librarian of how we should approach our user-centric work as we get involved in more remote activities in response to the internet age. For library management, it is hoped that the Five Rules can serve as a useful framework for training, building staff consensus, service evaluation and the induction of new staff in a user-centred library.

References

Antonacopoulou, E. P. and Guttel, W. H. (2010) Staff Induction Practices and Organizational Socialization: a review and extension of the debate, *Society and Business Review*, **5** (1), 22–47.

Choy, F. C. (2007) Libraries and Librarians – what next?, *Library Management*, **28** (3), 112–24.

Dunbar, R. I. M. (1992) Neocortex Size as a Constraint on Group Size in Primates, *Journal of Human Evolution*, **22** (6), 469–93.

Ranganathan, S. R. (1931) *The Five Laws of Library Science*, The Madras Library Association.

Stover, M. (2004) The Reference Librarian as Non-expert: a postmodern approach to expertise, *The Reference Librarian*, **87/88**, 273–300.

CHAPTER 4

Library management, disruption and consortia: an Australian example

Michael Robinson

Introduction: the value of library consortia

Library consortia navigate a course between providing benefit to their member institutions through a range of collaborative activities and opportunities and, in return, requiring financial and in-kind commitments to sustain the consortium. Deriving benefit from library collaboration usually entails obligations from each participant, such as long-term commitment to programmes, active engagement of library leadership and staff in the management and co-ordination of activities, and both direct and indirect financial commitments to the consortium and the programmes it operates on members' behalf.

The commitment implicit in any form of formal library collaboration can be twofold. On the one hand, members of a consortium have a commitment to the entity or organization set up to manage and co-ordinate a collaborative enterprise on their behalf, while on the other hand there is a commitment directly to the other participants in the collaborative activity. For example, a certain level of spending commitment may be required for a library to participate in a consortial acquisitions exercise, or a commitment to provide access to library collections may be a prerequisite of a collaborative resource-sharing or inter-lending programme. Such commitment may demand that a participating library undertake not just a share in the consortium's costs or management, but a degree of compromise and risk in committing and adhering to collaborative programmes and activities in the long term. Potentially, there is an inherent risk in collaboration, in so far as the object of the collaboration or the actions taken to achieve it may fail or may depart from the original aims. There is also a potential for compromise, in that an individual member may need to make concessions so as to accommodate the broader needs or interests of the group.

The value of collaborative library activity may also vary over time as the assumptions on which a joint enterprise is undertaken are undermined, for example, by systemic changes to the types of resources and services that the library offers and the way in which these are delivered, or by the opportunities that arise from technological or environmental changes and their potential to supersede the collaborative enterprise, or by the demands and imperatives set by parent institutions to demonstrate value and return on investment. While good faith is a fundamental of any library collaboration, tensions can arise if some types of collaborative activity may ultimately decline in value for one or more members as their own local needs, priorities and service models change or take precedence.

Consequently, the question arises as to how libraries should respond to these changes and pressures in the degree to which they engage – or remain engaged – in co-operative or collaborative activities. How do libraries view or manage these commitments when both their business model and the basis for collaboration are disrupted and challenged by systemic, organizational or fiscal changes? Is collaborative behaviour more or less attractive when libraries are placed under new pressures, and are libraries now beginning to view collaboration as less advantageous as their traditional resource and service models become less relevant? This chapter will offer some perspectives on drivers for and against collaboration in a disrupted library management environment and will draw examples from the member programmes and other service activities of the Australian library consortium CAVAL so as to discuss how consortia can frame their response through new opportunities and improved value.

Collaboration between Australian libraries

Australian libraries and librarians have for many years sought benefits for both their organizations and their users through collaborative activities. In the academic library sector, libraries share in the benefits offered through the programmes of the National Library of Australia, such as Libraries Australia and the Libraries Australia Document Delivery (LADD) services, and through the Council of Australian University Librarians (CAUL) and its work in areas such as consortial acquisitions, borrowing through the University Libraries in Australia and New Zealand (ULANZ) programme, and advocacy and policy development. There are also other state-level co-operative entities such as the Queensland University Libraries Office of Cooperation, University Libraries South Australia and the Western Australian Group of University Librarians. In other library sectors, similar consortial and collaborative arrangements have been in place for many years, for example through the National and State Libraries Association and local networks and consortia of public libraries, such as the Public Libraries Victoria Network.

These collaborative entities often pursue different missions and core activities, and both their value proposition and the basis on which they are funded and sustained also vary in each case. In some cases, such as with CAUL and a number of the state-based consortia, a substantial proportion of the cost is borne indirectly through the active management of programmes by the membership, for example in chairing and participating in the work of sub-committees or actively overseeing programmes. In addition, in some cases the nature of the consortial activity involved – such as acquisitions or resource-sharing programmes – enables many consortia to operate with relatively small secretariats or executive managements, jointly funded through membership fees or contributions.

CAVAL and UNILINC

Other collaborations, however, are managed by entities established in their own right and operate as member-based organizations – engaged with and accountable to their memberships for various programmes – while also undertaking fee-for-service activities that are available to the library sector as a whole and that help to fund and sustain the organization. In the Australian academic library sector, UNILINC (a not-for-profit library co-operative) and CAVAL are prominent examples of this approach. UNILINC is based in Sydney, New South Wales, and over many years has successfully developed a mix of member services and fee-for-service activities in areas such as library systems management, cataloguing and processing services and consultancy work (Wade and Horton, 2014). CAVAL (which initially stood for Co-operative Action by Victorian Academic Libraries) was established at approximately the same time (in the late 1970s) and is based in Melbourne, Victoria. CAVAL was founded as a co-operative by Victorian university libraries and its original aim was to explore and undertake activities of mutual interest and benefit to its members, providing opportunities for innovation, service and resource development, and efficiencies through economies of scale. Since then, CAVAL's mission has evolved to include fee-for-service activities of benefit to the Australian and New Zealand library community in general. The consortium thus performs a dual role by continuing to develop services collaboratively with its members, while also pursuing new or expanded fee-for-service activities for benefit within the wider Australian and New Zealand library sector.

Historically, CAVAL's most successful and enduring member collaborative ventures have been based on the sharing of print resources. The first of these is the CAVAL Reciprocal Borrowing Program, which since the early 1980s has provided the staff and students of member institutions with a practical means of borrowing in person from the substantial print collections of all participating libraries, a resource comprising several million volumes. In 1996, CAVAL established its original CARM (CAVAL Archival and Research Materials) Centre as a shared off-site storage facility of last-copy materials deposited by member libraries, and today the CARM Shared Collection comprises over 800,000 volumes, forming a research collection held in perpetuity for the use of current and future generations of scholars (Jilovsky, 2013). In addition to this, CAVAL supports a number of member interest groups and activities, and works with these groups to organize programmes of mutual interest, providing networking and professional development opportunities for member-library staff.

In addition, CAVAL has progressively expanded the range of services that it offers on a fee-for-service basis, fundamentally with the aim of achieving self-sufficiency through the income generated by these activities, but also to engage in activities that complement and support its member programmes. It is perhaps best known in the library community for its cataloguing services in over 70 different languages (including English) for academic and public libraries, as well as training and professional development programmes, library consultancies and the compilation and management of the annual CAUL statistical database for all Australian and New Zealand university libraries. Since 2004, however, the portfolio has grown to include the shelf-ready supply of Languages Other Than English (LOTE) books and other resources, the support of library resource-sharing systems, provision of digitizing services and support for library-security and book-handling systems. In response to members' interest in a flexible print storage option as well as long-term projections for demand for print storage, in 2010 CAVAL established CARM2 as one of its major commercial undertakings. Although similar in design to the original CARM1, this second purpose-built storage facility is fundamentally different in its business model, in so far as it offers short- and long-term storage services for libraries and other cultural institutions on a commercially leased basis, and has become one of the core CAVAL fee-for-service businesses (Wright, Jilovsky and Anderson, 2012).

Key challenges to collaborative behaviour
Delivery of digital information products

Since the early 1990s, academic libraries have steadily moved away from a predominantly print-based custodial and service role to one focused on the delivery of digital information products, learning and support services. Concurrently, academic libraries have been placed under greater financial pressures by their institutions and have sought greater effectiveness and efficiency in the type of resources they provide and how they are delivered to the university community. In addition, there has been a greater emphasis in general on improving accountability and demonstrating return on investment, this scrutiny being applied both internally to the products and services offered by the library and externally to the services it supports in collaboration with others. Consequently, set against this background, it is perhaps inevitable and necessary that the assumptions behind the value of library collaboration should be revisited.

By way of illustration, for most of CAVAL's existence the benefit of membership of the consortium was virtually unquestioned, as the services it provided or co-ordinated were closely aligned with the traditional print resource management and service-delivery models of its academic library membership. The CAVAL Reciprocal Borrowing Program, for example, has historically been central to the value proposition of the consortium, as it provided a means for students and staff of member institutions to borrow in person from the print collections of other member libraries, and did so more quickly and economically than traditional inter-library loan (ILL) services. It also complemented the libraries' heavy reliance on print resources and lending as the basis of their service delivery, enhanced the value of the investment in print and offered opportunities to access a greater volume of material than could otherwise be provided locally. The business case for the other key CAVAL member service – the CARM Shared Collection – has likewise been built fundamentally around the management of print, as it is predicated on a steady rate of deposit of materials from member libraries and of continued retrieval from the collection overall. Many CAVAL fee-or-service activities are also essentially print based, for example its long-standing cataloguing and shelf-ready processing services, which are targeted at print materials from the collections and new acquisitions of member and non-member libraries alike. In addition, other products and services, such as digitizing, the support of ILL and document delivery software (DDS) and the sale of library security and book-dispensing equipment, are also based in one form or another on the handling of print.

This contrasts with trends in the Australian academic library sector that reflect the decline in prominence of the printed book as the basic unit of currency for information provision. There has been, for example, a general decrease in the volume of print monographs acquired by academic libraries and a corresponding increasing investment in e-book monographs and textbooks. Declines in print acquisition rates have both reflected and contributed to equally pronounced decreases in the level of print borrowing in Australian academic libraries. While there are many ramifications of these changes for the libraries individually in their mode of service delivery, there have been noticeable effects on consortial print management services as well, reflected in particular in the decline in the shared use of print resources. Since at least 2005, for example, the number of loans generated through the CAVAL Reciprocal Borrowing Program has declined by almost two-thirds. This decline is consistent with the decline in print usage recorded internally within the member libraries as their communities find more accessible alternatives in the digital domain.

Unmediated inter-lending systems

Traditional walk-in borrowing services have also been disrupted by more convenient technologies to facilitate access to print materials. Chief among these in the context of collaborative resource sharing has been the advent of patron-initiated unmediated inter-lending systems. These enable the library user to request an item from another participating library via their library's discovery layer and to have the item dispatched to them for borrowing locally. This challenges the walk-in reciprocal borrowing model by providing an alternative that does not require the user to travel to retrieve the item, nor to undertake separate borrower registration processes in order to access the library. In the Australian context, the establishment and growth of the BONUS+ network of 14 academic libraries since 2004 has demonstrated the appeal of this mode of service delivery for print materials, and has also to some extent displaced traditional reciprocal borrowing services provided by CAVAL (Anderson and Wilson, 2010).

The CAVAL model for its CARM Shared Collection is predicated on the establishment and guaranteed retention of a last-copy volume from the collections of its members. Its value as off-site collective storage is that it not only ensures the accessibility of the print copy regardless of changes in the member libraries, but it also enables the membership to make collection management choices more freely in the knowledge that a copy is available. Access to the shared collection also addresses possible concerns of academic staff at member institutions about the potential for the irretrievable loss of valuable or historical research collections (Jilovsky and Genoni, 2014). However, maintenance of this collection and the facility in which it is housed is one of the major cost drivers for CAVAL, and the same trends witnessed in publishing and delivery that are leading to declines in the use of print resources both within academic libraries and in resource-sharing schemes are also impacting on the rationale for the long-term repository storage of print. The increasing availability of both current and historical materials in digital form and the increasing adoption of 'e-preferred' acquisitions policies challenge the concept of long-term print storage, as it is anticipated that the ingress of print materials into storage may decline and that the collection itself may also become redundant.

Changing commitments to collaboration

How, then, do libraries view or manage their commitments to collaborative behaviour when their own service models are subject to the impacts of long-term transition from print to digital? In addition, is collaboration seen as inherently more risky or extravagant when library managers are also responding to more demanding fiscal and accountability environments? While inevitably the answers to these questions will differ according to the type of consortium, its membership and the services it manages on their behalf, the CAVAL experience has been – and continues to be – one of transforming its product and service mix to retain its relevance to the needs of both its immediate membership and the library sector in general.

Shaping the Shared Collection

Demonstrating relevance to academic library missions can exhibit itself in different ways. For example, while there may be debate concerning the long-term relevance of the CAVAL Shared Collection to a digital library service environment, this tends to focus at present on the composition of the collection itself, rather than on the concept of off-site shared storage in general. This debate focuses more on the depth of research content in the Shared Collection that is likely to be of intrinsic value to future generations of scholars. While collection-analysis studies have been undertaken in the past (Genoni and Varga, 2009), the interest of the membership has shifted to some extent to what needs to be retained into the future so as to satisfy research needs, while also taking into account the increasing availability of more accessible electronic versions. Shaping the Shared Collection for the future also needs to consider claims that e-publishing has not yet reached the level at which all or even a substantial majority of titles are published electronically in addition to or instead of in print. It is argued that an over-reliance on the e-copy equates to an over-reliance on the commercial organizations that maintain and sell access to e-content, and that in general these organizations offer no guarantees as to the retention and maintenance of all of their e-content in perpetuity. With a view to the long-term future, some member libraries therefore contend that abandoning print storage is not responsible stewardship of institutional resources for the long-term benefit of future generations of scholarship. Consequently, instead of questioning the rationale for the collection overall, effort is being invested into determining whether the materials being held reflect the original intent and purpose of the Shared Collection, and how the value and relevance of the collection might be improved to align with existing and future needs of the CAVAL membership.

In addition, acknowledging that libraries may ultimately adopt different approaches to the management of legacy print collections, ranging from collaborative storage solutions through to the maintenance of steady-state print collections and disposal of volumes superseded by electronic equivalents, CAVAL is seeking to widen the scope of its shared storage solutions through greater rather than less collaborative effort. In particular, there is the potential to establish a coalition of Australian libraries and other institutions committed to the long-term storage of print on a distributed national basis (Anderson, 2012). The potential threat to collaborative storage posed by disruption to library print services therefore also presents opportunities for CAVAL to engage with a greater consortium of libraries committed to a shared last-copy retention model.

Reciprocal borrowing programmes

In a similar vein, the gradual decline in the use of the CAVAL Reciprocal Borrowing Program has acted as a catalyst not for the winding up of the programme, but for its expansion and diversification. As noted above, use of the Reciprocal Borrowing Program has been decreasing at least since 2005, partly as a consequence of there being less reliance on print, but also to some extent because of displacement by other book-requesting and delivery systems. While its current level of use demonstrates that the service remains highly valued by the user communities of its members, CAVAL is integrating the existing in-person service with an unmediated requesting and delivery system to transact loan requests and fulfilments between participating libraries, optimizing choice for the user in the way in which they access print materials and aligning this programme more closely with the service offerings of member libraries. As this system uses the NISO Circulation Interchange Protocol (NCIP) to conduct searches and transactions, it is interoperable between libraries with different management systems and, as such, has the potential to develop into a wider, quasi-national network of academic libraries beyond the immediate CAVAL membership. Paradoxically, rather than the walk-in Reciprocal

Borrowing Program being eclipsed by enabling technologies, this may potentially lead to a scaling up rather than down of print lending between academic libraries (Jilovsky and Robinson, 2015).

Flexible storage solutions

While the above concerns show how specific collaborative activities remain relevant to the changing missions and needs of participating libraries, systemic disruption to academic libraries provides opportunities in other ways as libraries seek new shared efficiencies from their consortia. Paradoxically, while the CAVAL business model centred on the stewardship of print appears to be at odds with the new priorities of the libraries it supports, it is precisely in this role that clear growth opportunities exist. The same drivers of change that have been propelling Australian academic libraries into a preferred digital acquisitions and delivery model are also encouraging greater degrees of collaborative behaviour in the managing of remaining print collections and print-dependent services. For example, in transforming former physical collection areas into a range of learning spaces, both member and non-member academic libraries are seeking flexible solutions for the decanting and retention of print collections. As an alternative to commitment to in-perpetuity shared storage, these libraries are turning to CAVAL to lease storage space for an indeterminate period, affording the library flexibility in determining the long-term future of its stored print collections. The libraries retain ownership and, therefore, the decision about how long and in what way to house materials, and this in turn has given rise to a number of client-driven storage solutions being developed, ranging in duration from a few months through to three decades or more.

As libraries continue to evaluate what needs to be accessible and on site in the mix of print and digital services they offer their communities, new opportunities also arise for the consortium as a trusted third party to take on a greater share in the stewardship of library resources. This might entail an increasing involvement in the storage of collections, such as rare and special collections, mandatory deposits and donations, and residual non-print formats such as microfilm. It may also apply to the upstream management of library operations such as acquisitions, cataloguing, processing and other activities as libraries seek efficiencies through the devolution of in-house operations. For CAVAL, opportunities to play a stronger and more direct role in the management of library print collections exist in its capacity to offer combinations of its technical services (such as cataloguing and serials management) and storage operations to manage and store library collections in a variety of ways. This could also extend to active collection management services within the libraries themselves, for example in the provision of collection analysis, deselection and processing of materials destined for off-site storage. CAVAL has for many years offered cataloguing services to academic and public libraries, specializing in the niche activity of LOTE cataloguing. However, as libraries divest themselves of print resources and the services that support them – often in response to strong financial imperatives to scale down operations – they are looking to CAVAL to outsource a greater range of functions. The first of these has been for the cataloguing service to expand to take in academic English as well as LOTE cataloguing, and this has in turn been extended to the provision of shelf-ready processing services. This has since led to new initiatives in the management and processing of academic library print serials and in other niche areas such as audiovisual materials.

The demand for these types of services from CAVAL as a third party in preference to in-house management of these activities is indicative of a positive and outward-looking attitude to the stewardship model. To continue to remain relevant, however, CAVAL needs to re-shape its services and infrastructure to collaborative opportunities in the digital environment also. This entails not only transitioning existing services such as cataloguing to support the management of digital as well as print resources, but exploring and developing solutions for emerging academic library needs and priorities. One such area where members are seeking a collaborative response is in the development of systems for the compilation, analysis and interpretation of e-content. With heavy and increasing investment in digital over print, libraries need a stronger evidence base to support decision making and to demonstrate the value of the products and services they provide. Seeing this as a problem requiring a joint solution rather than one for a library to attempt on its own restates the value proposition of the consortial approach. It enables libraries to address issues that they might not otherwise have the resources to deal with individually, it promotes and facilitates innovation and it offers the prospect of developing services of mutual interest in an efficient and sustainable way.

Conclusion: the value proposition of collaboration

The examples provided here of one Australian consortium illustrate that, if anything, libraries are looking more towards collaboration for support as they continue to make the transition away from services centred on local print collections and transactions and towards engagement with their users on a network scale. As for similar organizations in Australia and around the world, significant collaborative opportunities continue to exist for CAVAL through shared efficiencies in the management of print collections, as well as in the future management of digital content. The same changes and pressures that disrupt the traditional print service model can also be drivers for libraries to seek efficiencies in all aspects of the stewardship of print and other physical resources (and, indeed, in the management of some aspects of their digital content) through outsourcing and collaborative activity. Likewise, the challenges to print-based resource-sharing activities among libraries – typically print storage and reciprocal borrowing – also create opportunities for greater rather than less collaboration to achieve economies of scale through the improved management and co-ordination of print collections regionally or nationally, and improved access through integrated discovery, lending and delivery systems. While apparently posing threats to the future of the consortium, a number of current trends also present opportunities and may ultimately encourage stronger, rather than weaker, collaborative behaviour.

References

Anderson, C. (2012) Rethinking Resource Sharing: the case for a shared national research collection, *Australian Library and Information Association (ALIA) Biennial Conference*, Sydney, Australia.

Anderson, G. and Wilson, K. (2010) It's a BONUS Plus! Collaborating to share library resources across Australasia, *Australian Library and Information Association (ALIA) Access Conference*, Brisbane, Australia.

Genoni, P. and Varga, E. (2009) Assessing the Potential for a National Print Repository: results of an Australian overlap study, *College and Research Libraries*, **70** (6), 555–67.

Jilovsky, C. (2013) The CARM Centre: the creation, revelation and evolution of a print repository, *Australian Academic and Research Libraries*, **44** (2), 113–24.

Jilovsky, C. and Genoni, P. (2014) Shared Collections to Shared Storage: the CARM1 and CARM2 print repositories, *Library Management*, **35** (1/2), 2–14.

Jilovsky, C. and Robinson, M. (2015) Discovery to Delivery: enabling an
    unmediated resource discovery and delivery service in a collaborative context,
    ALIA Online Conference, Sydney, Australia (forthcoming).
Wade, R. and Horton, V. (2014) Collaboration in Australian Library Consortia,
    Collaborative Librarianship, **6** (1), 47–9.
Wright, J., Jilovsky, C. and Anderson, C. (2012) The Story of a Shared Last
    Copy Repository in Australia: the CARM Centre Stage 2 development,
    Collection Management, **37**, 271–93.

CHAPTER 5

No regrets; just lessons: economic crisis is changing our life and the management of libraries

Petros A. Kostagiolas

Introduction: library management and the global economic crisis

This chapter attempts to take a global, or at least a European, look at the effects of the economic crisis on the dominant, market-driven approaches to library management and at the underlying socio-economic aspects of that crisis. Throughout history, library administrators and managers have certainly demonstrated an active interest in socio-economic and technological change and crisis. The risks and threats posed to libraries and library collections are typically related to natural causes (earthquakes, floods, etc.) and to human-related disasters (epidemics and wars, terrorism, etc.) resulting from political and social instability. Economic crises, however, have deep philosophical roots, are difficult to predict and even harder to understand (Greene and McMenemy, 2012). This is so in the case of the global economic crisis of 2008, which hit not only libraries but also their dominant underlying library management principles with full force. Indeed, although a number of studies are available (see Kostagiolas et al., 2013, for a review) on the effects of economic crisis on library services and their operations, very few, if any, actually deal with the impact of economic crisis on the library management paradigm itself. Lessons can be learned from the current economic crisis in terms of the role and the socio-economic positioning of libraries, and obviously the 'proper' after-crisis library management still needs to be detailed, elaborated and analysed.

This chapter offers a contribution to discussions on the reassessment of the underlying values of library and information services management in the face of economic crisis. This management notion should aim to guide and actually prepare libraries to respond in financially straitened times. For the present analysis, it is not considered necessary to provide detailed definitions of economic (or fiscal) crises or even to detail the literature on the causes of the different types of crises. However, everyone dealing with library management will agree that a deep economic recession can bring about catastrophic socio-economic events that may cause shock to libraries. For example, public library administration will be in a distressed condition when state funding is reduced by 80% in three fiscal years and staffing levels are dramatically reduced. While staffing reductions as a result of fiscal constraints and corresponding library budget reductions are terrible for those who have lost their jobs, at the same time there are also negative consequences to the library science profession as a whole, in terms of research, quality of library service provision and library management. Furthermore, those who are lucky enough to retain their jobs may suffer significant reductions in their annual income and an overall worsening in their employment conditions. In Greece, for example, much of the newly introduced 'activity' in libraries has been realized through low-paid short-term employment contracts.

Within Europe the economic crisis of 2008 hit the weaker economies of the south (Portugal, Greece, Spain, Italy etc.) first of all, and assumed different quantitative and qualitative characteristics and trajectories in other countries and/or economic sectors. However, generally speaking, the current crisis has become established in people's minds as a 'global bank-driven economic crisis' with political and social ramifications, e.g. for the role of the European integration mechanisms, bank-monitoring systems and other international funding mechanisms. Most of us, irrespective of our role and educational background, accept that the economic crisis exists and will continue for the foreseeable future. This has a very real and direct impact on decision making in libraries, and has forced policy makers and managers to reconsider the economic positioning of cultural heritage organizations (Demoule, 2010; Schlanger and Aitchison, 2010) and libraries. Clearly, what may be quite important for the future is the realization that many existing management practices, processes and patterns failed to predict and respond to the economic crisis. As scholars and researchers in library management we need to admit that the crisis found us vulnerable and exposed to economic threats. This is mostly related to the 'secure' consumerist management culture and the underlying principles that drive library management. We need to acknowledge that library management education and library management curricula need to take account of the lessons provided by the economic crisis, in order to better prepare future library professionals and leaders.

Internationally, as well as in Europe, in different countries the library profession has distinct customs, management cultures and systems and state-intervention mechanisms. However, the economic crisis has provided a novel and interesting lens through which to understand the after-crisis library management paradigm. The economic crisis is indeed a complex socio-economic phenomenon and a return to 'normality' in library management may first require far-reaching change and theoretical reorientation. Our starting hypothesis is that the impacts of the economic crisis (see, e.g., Mostad-Jensen, 2009) suggest the need for a reorganization of the decision-making mechanisms in libraries, i.e. an after-crisis library management paradigm based on modern management techniques but driven by professional regulations and values. The 'art' of managing information organizations needs to be thought through carefully and to take account of traditional professional values (Broady-Preston and Cox, 2000). Although the details are rather uncertain, the direction is to appreciate the 'true' value of libraries (Holt, 2007) as creators of intellectual and social capital that needs to be put ahead of economic, market-driven concepts of 'blind' individualism and consumerism. The fact is that during economically straitened times, when the economic criteria prevail, libraries' budgets shrink, their personnel are cut and the quality of their services declines dramatically. On the other hand, when economic crisis is viewed as an opportunity for change, an innovative 'back to the future' professional culture can enable libraries to create value in terms of socio-economic support activities and services that have a positive impact on levels of employment, productivity, coherence and well-being.

To this end, the rest of this chapter is organized as follows: the next section discusses the effectiveness of dominant management concepts and their underlying socio-economic dilemmas. By the means of a review of selected literature, the impact of 'blind', market-driven policies is discussed vis-à-vis a library management role that is based on non-consumerist values and the creation of social value. Misconceptions of the role of public investment are discussed and the concept of the library as a merit good and service is presented. Socially driven meta-marketing in libraries is introduced, along with the identification, measurement and management of intellectual-capital resources. The third section presents an agenda for developing a new management paradigm based on the lessons learnt from the current economic crisis, while the final section presents some conclusions.

No regrets: global 'views' of underlying principles of library management

The management of memory institutions, cultural heritage organizations and library and information services encapsulates socio-economic ideologies regarding the way that people perceive our global information and knowledge heritage as well as the way in which we prioritize the management forces 'driving' these organizations. The management culture of Western mixed economies is underpinned by two broad, socio-economic and politically sensitive perspectives with regard to the principal role of the state (or other regulatory authorities) or the principal role of the market: the first is a management perspective drawn from the regulation-driven, neo-Keynesian school; the second is an individualistic, neoliberal, market-driven perspective. These two contrasting concepts affect the way that libraries (and other cultural heritage organizations) are financed, the way they see their users as citizens, consumers or customers, etc., and the way their services are designed and offered. Overall, these underlying ideologies have an impact on the way libraries and information services are perceived and managed (Clarke, 2007).

Over the last decades globalization, which is mainly based on the capitalist and neoliberal principles of individualism, consumerism and privatization, has had an impact on the way libraries are managed (Greene and McMenemy, 2012). The adoption of market-oriented values and private sector management techniques in the library sector has been studied extensively (Panda and Mandal, 2006; Aharony, 2009). However, this influence of neoliberal management in library and information services (LIS) has been criticized as mimicking the private sector without adaptation to and consideration of the special needs of the LIS area (Usherwood, 2007; McMenemy, 2009). Greene and McMenemy (2012) provide an interesting review of the literature on the impact of neoliberal ideas on public librarianship, along five strands:

(1) Commodification of public librarianship ('blinded' application of market principles and implementation of consumerist postures)
(2) Managerialism and public libraries (application of a 'rationalizing' return-on-investment economic management culture)
(3) Deprofessionalization (commercialization versus the traditional professional values)
(4) Citizen-consumers (management based on a consumerist society and culture, with the notion of citizens as consumers of public services)
(5) Modernity and the use of language (neoliberal principles provide a terminology for modernization versus the 'anachronistic' terminology of professionals).

The same authors identify and report neoliberal narratives in statements from public libraries. The underlying 'ideology' of library management is indeed a very interesting avenue for research and needs to be better linked to the economic crisis.

Dominant neoliberal management solutions, 'blind' consumerism and the dissolution of the public realm have been put to test during the economic crisis. Management reformations in libraries have not been ideologically related to the traditional 'altruistic', 'equality of access' professional values (Usherwood, 2007), and commercialism has been adopted in the name of economic 'rationalization' and efficiency. A study of the management of libraries and other cultural organizations cannot be conducted solely through the economic lens of the private sector. Throughout their long history these organizations have been related to the public sphere (Buschman, 2005), generating a higher-order positive impact through education, promotion of literacy, dissemination of information etc., and serving the common good as valuable components of a functioning society, economy and democracy. Libraries and information services utilize and create intellectual and social capital (Kostagiolas and Asonitis, 2011) the value of which can be only partially estimated using traditional economic techniques, and therefore require distinct management approaches (Kostagiolas, 2012). The professional values that underpin the development of policies and library management actions take account of the library's role as a representative of the community of citizens (Goulding, 2006).

For example, a number of simplistic library 'valuators' or value calculators based on the commodification of public librarianship have been made available that attempt to assign an economic value to library services (Missingham, 2005) and thus to provide a public sense of return on investment (Kostagiolas, 2012). These 'valuators' function by the means of a financial estimation worksheet introduced by the Maine[1] State Library for estimating the 'savings' (see below) made by a library user per month. The calculator has been presented by the American Library Association and adopted by the Massachusetts Library Association[2] and quite a few others. However, the 'true' value of the public library goes beyond such restricted economic estimations. It encompasses the creation of social capital (Varheim, 2009) and contributes to the development of intellectual capital in the economy and in society as a whole (Ramírez, 2010). Criticism of value calculators includes the fact that they are restricted to a superficial, user-savings viewpoint and hence they cannot be used for library costing or pricing. Library calculators are restricted to a myopic view of economic value, ignoring all aspects of intellectual capital that make the library experience unique for each user (Kostagiolas, 2012). One could argue (erroneously) that library value estimators 'explain' the increasing demand for public library services during periods of economic crisis as being due solely to the reduced income of the 'consumers' and the 'replacement' of private expense by information 'commodities' (e.g. books, scholarly material, access to electronic services). However, we librarians who have experienced the economic crisis in the period after October 2008 recognize the importance of libraries during the crisis as providers of a wide array of information goods, offered to a community of citizens (not consumers) and directly related to their real-life issues such as unemployment, health-care information, information literacy skills etc. Indeed, the public library provides an 'experience' to its users through a complex personal dialogue with the information space and the collective memory.

As Kyrillidou (2010) sophisticatedly suggests on the issue of library value:

> We hold these truths to be self-evident: libraries are valuable to humankind; libraries preserve knowledge; libraries enable access to information; libraries

serve the information needs of their users. To the believer the truth is evident. But libraries are not natural phenomena like the sun rising and setting every day. Libraries are institutions created and supported by those individuals who hold that these statements are true even if not self-evident to everyone.

The 'user savings' as computed by library valuators include only a restricted and consumerist perspective of value that is based primarily on cost avoidance. A generic list of prices is created in order to show how much money a user can save or has saved by using the library rather than paying for the materials borrowed or the questions asked (Germano, 2011). Such valuations represent only a portion of the *true* value that the library produces. Town (2010) suggests that the concept of a 'transcendent library' may provide a route to further progress in the valuation of library services and identify organizational and social values, rather than simply a narrow notion of economic value. The author proposes a value-scorecard approach, incorporating both the value and the impact of transcendent libraries, in which 'the value can be judged beyond immediate needs and demands, through contribution to less concrete aspects of institutional or societal intent'. This is, of course, different from the management paradigm of private companies, which is driven by the 'hidden hand' of their shareholders, who prefer immediate tangible profits rather than the benefits resulting from long-term investment.

Misconceptions on public and private investment in libraries: managing library services as merit goods

During times of economic crisis those who support privatization of the public sector raise concerns about the so-called 'low productivity' of the public sector and a bureaucracy with excessively complicated administrative procedures. In the case of public libraries, however, the 'low productivity' concern has not been validated by any study that is known to us, nor has any efficiency benchmarking comparison of private and public libraries been available. The role of the public sector is often perilously misinterpreted by camouflaging the positive impacts of public investments to the private sector. There is also the potential for concurrent co-operation (Enser, 2001) with private institutions through 'co-opetitive' (co-operative competition) information networks.

Library services should be evaluated beyond the criteria of short-term economic efficiency and should be managed as a public or common good (e.g. Underwood, 1990) through their long-lasting professional values as a service 'provided for all'. The theory of public goods (Musgrave, 1969) suggests that if information services constitute an asset to the private sector they cannot always be offered for free (e.g. Kirk, 1999); and they can sometimes be produced or provided by the private sector on behalf of the public sector. In general, public goods and services are defined as those services that the private sector either fails to produce at all or finds it difficult to produce efficiently in order to generate a profit. In other words, public goods are those services that the market fails to produce, owing to its inherent weaknesses. Public goods are characterized (Musgrave, 1969) by their:

1   common or non-competitive use (non-rivalry), i.e. the use of an information service by an additional user does not affect the benefits that other, simultaneous users enjoy when using the library infrastructure
2   inability to exclude those users who refuse or fail to pay (non-excludable)
3   inability to discontinue the use of particular services.

Within this framework, any effort to exclude any category of user from the use of a particular good, in this case the information service, would be unacceptable. The first two distinctive features of public goods are easily discernible for library services. The third (the inability of users to alter the use of public goods) shares some characteristics with the classic examples of national defence and police services. Private goods are those services that serve purely private needs. Services of this kind are part of the total equation. It is possible to exclude certain users, should they fail to meet the demands of pricing policy.

In the face of the pressure of economic recession, a 'user pays' principle (even if users themselves could agree on a minimal fee) would have certain drawbacks.

First, since nobody is excluded from the benefits provided by a library, any third party (legal entity or a person) can actually try to avoid paying his contribution in order to decrease his own expenses (production or life). Indeed, if more users follow such a course (according to the anthropological features that neoclassical theory has bestowed on *homo economicus*), then a minimum-fee 'user pays' policy will fail. This was the case in Greece, for example, where some municipal and institutional libraries suffered extreme budget reductions, due to users' refusal to pay the agreed but non-obligatory fees. Of course, this behaviour was a result of the terrible economic and fiscal crisis, and it resulted in library mergers in order to improve the efficiency of municipal expenditure. Further, the service productivity of a library is not unlimited, and so an opportunity is created for those who use its resources the more. This is a 'congestion' phenomenon, which will considerably decrease the availability of services to those who need such services (Samuelson, 1954).

Second, library services tend gradually to become regulated by international professional associations, library networks and links, and political and economical unions (e.g. the European Union), thus providing a framework for their management and provision. Therefore, investments in library services are a mixture of public and private sector, which makes them a merit good. Merit goods constitute a category of service that is provided mostly by public organizations, because the private sector will not easily or readily take action for their development. However, during the economic crisis the problem of reduced public investment, combined with a wide range of other issues, has driven library managers to seek opportunities for additional funding. The objective is to develop a regulatory framework that will help management to secure the principle of 'library access for all' and at the same time pass an obligatory proportion of library service and production costs to those private sector users who use the library's services for their own profit.

A significant obstacle to the participation of private capital in information services investment may be the absence of any overt economic incentive for such private investment. Nowadays several investments in libraries and information services have features that render them not particularly attractive to the private sector. Only a small proportion of these can be regarded as profitable (especially in a period of economic crisis), such that they yield returns that amortize the initial capital or loan and offer a desirable level of profit. These factors indicate that public discourse on private sector participation in the production of information services should not proceed in a sentimental, dogmatic or short-sighted manner. While it is surely possible to fully privatize a library and retain a regulatory role for a specified authority (e.g. a national library or the state), it is likely that such a privatization would drive the library to make further cutbacks. What on the contrary is expected to happen in a number of libraries is to have the possibility of producing a wide, innovative mix of services in co-operation with both the public and the private sphere. It is a fact that to achieve growth during economic crisis is very difficult; however, in the case of libraries, many forms of regulated investment should be thoroughly studied, including the experience of private–public-sector partnerships in different countries.

Irreproachable meta-marketing for library services

Marketing is a philosophy of making decisions based on the study and description of transactions, and investigates the efficient economic strategy of value supply in the direction of desirable change, i.e. profit. Marketing in the private sector may be characterized as an effort towards commercial/consumerist mastery and takes the form of a multifaceted strategy that governs the entirety of operations in an enterprise. At a first glance, marketing practices and activities seem to relate only to the private sector (Kotler, 1972). In recent years marketing, market research and promotion-advertising have tended to be released from exclusive application in the private sector and industrial capital. Such approaches have been developed since the World War 2 period, drawing elements from social sciences. The redirection of marketing has intensified, because of the pressures exerted on organizations by increasing international competition. This has been due to the transition of developed countries' economies from production- and transaction-based economies to citizens' relationship-based economies and the direction taken by the 'new' economy (Elsner, 2004). Marketing as a philosophical approach has followed this trend, attempting to shape a framework of theories, methods and practices for the 'socialization' of business operations and the moulding of closer relationships between stakeholders.

The effort to develop or maintain this transactional relationship with regard to products, services, organizations, individuals, places or purposes nowadays constitutes 'meta-marketing', which also comprises approaches to corporate ethics as well as corporate social responsibility and corporate social accountability. The main ideological constant of the 'marketing *is* society' orientation of meta-marketing is that the user and society are the supreme and final judges of those who produce services (Sherry, 2013). The transfer of power to the final user reinforces the theoretical possibility of rejection as an option for 'free' users in the market. The research approach to meta-marketing, dictating that the 'business' should investigate the expectations and needs of users, thereby sharing the burden of wider socio-economic needs, calls for particular caution. For this reason a unique meta-marketing approach for libraries is needed so as to safeguard the general interests of the public with regard to a given merit good (library service) while at the same time ensuring the balanced development of services. Approaches of this type can provide a theoretical basis for the study of regulated library services, for which there should be a special meta-marketing and management.

The developing library public relations and meta-marketing programmes applications (Neuhaus and Snowden, 2003) are characteristic examples. In the definition of meta-marketing strategy for libraries, a rough prediction of demand is taken into account, together with methods for an optimal provision of services, promotion techniques, maintenance of information sources in perpetuity etc. In effect, planning for the production and provision of information services must encompass all necessary information, such that the needs, expectations and demands of individual users can be studied and the 'value' of information services as a merit good in society and in the economy can be considered. As a final point, to return to our preoccupation with the current global economic crisis, it should be mentioned that the effects of such a crisis on libraries and information services are quite different and more challenging than is the case for other public bodies operating under the same socio-economic conditions.

Intellectual capital management 'comes to the rescue' of library budgets

The term 'intellectual capital' is defined as the totality of intangible assets (or resources), which includes all the invisible, non-monetary assets/resources held by a library that have been amassed over time, that are not included in the balance sheet and that can be identified and analysed separately (Kaufman and Schneider, 2004; Kostagiolas and Asonitis, 2009). Some researchers prefer the term 'resources', since intellectual capital cannot always be 'owned' as any other 'private asset' by a library and therefore cannot be referred to as an 'asset', at least, not in the financial sense (Kostagiolas, 2012). A popular categorization of intellectual capital includes (Choong, 2008; Kostagiolas and Asonitis,

2009): (1) human capital, (2) organizational (or structural) capital and (3) relational capital. Human capital is related to personnel and includes the knowledge, experience, competencies and creativity of the staff. Structural capital includes the organizational structure, management system, information systems and patents; relational capital is defined as the relations that a library holds with its external environment (i.e. providers, users, other libraries and organizations etc.).

White (2007) suggested that the identification of intellectual capital in a library provides three benefits for the management team, in the form of:

1   reporting the library's effectiveness to stakeholders
2   unifying the library's tangible and intangible resources in order to meet the requirements of stakeholders
3   utilizing the library's intangibles in order to achieve its strategic objectives.

Similarly, Livonen and Huotari (2007) analysed the intellectual capital of an academic library, while Kostagiolas and Asonitis (2009 and 2011) have discussed the practical and theoretical issues of the subject. Asonitis and Kostagiolas (2010) proposed a methodological framework, based on the Analytic Hierarchy Process method, for establishing a hierarchy of value creation among the different intellectual capital resources of a library. Kostagiolas (2012) provides an extensive review of intellectual capital in libraries and information services. Roos, Pike and Fernström (2005) suggest that intellectual capital management is the 'deployment and management of intellectual capital resources and their transformations (into intellectual capital resources or into traditional capital resources) to maximize the present value of the organization's value creation in the eyes of its stakeholders'. Investments in intellectual capital resources/assets aim to create added value, which is shared among the organization's stakeholders, increasing the overall contribution to the community (Kostagiolas, 2012). Hence, the management team should regard intangibles as critical assets/resources that need to be identified, measured and eventually financially evaluated. Overall, the more its available intangible resources are managed within a memory institution, the greater the potential for diversification in the face of competition.

Although the contribution of intellectual capital to value creation within museums, libraries and other cultural heritage organizations is rather obvious, there is little information in the literature about identifying and measuring intellectual capital (Kostagiolas, 2012). Mobilizing additional resources during an economic crisis is quite important (Kostagiolas et al., 2013). It seems, however, that there is no single, commonly accepted framework for the identification and measurement of intangible library resources. The intellectual capital assets/resources should be identified and measured by means of specific indexes related to them and their contribution to the library (Gallego and Rodríguez, 2005), while management actions need to be decided for the mobilization of intangible resources so as to create value. These actions can lead to the creation of further intellectual capital or the assessment of previous investments. An appropriate framework will measure specific intangible assets/resources and their contribution to strategic goals. For example, the structural capital related to teamwork and flexible work practices can be measured and assessed in terms of their perceived contribution to achieving strategic goals, such as increasing the numbers of visits to a museum etc.

Lessons learnt: overview of a 'new' library management agenda?

The economic crisis has many facets and the failure of the dominant, market-driven management techniques necessitates the design of 'incentive-compatible' remedial management mechanisms (Ferguson, 2008). It is not only management that is changing, but our collective awareness, through new, interesting discussions. Clearly, following the economic crisis of 2008 a shift has been observed in the international debates among economists and policy makers about the impact of the crisis and how to respond to it (Farrell and Quiggin, 2012). The agendas of experts, as well as of other individuals and decision makers, include rethinking the dominant loose and unreliable consumerist perspective on the management of the libraries. These systems of library management have failed to respond capably and innovatively, and inevitably have been insufficient to provide the proper 'leading fibre' required by society during the economic crisis.

Of course, despite their uniqueness, libraries are organizations with resources that need to be managed, and they cannot avoid pressures from the external environment, including, in some cases, harsh socio-economic realities (Kostagiolas, 2012). Understandably, people all over the world are greatly concerned with the economic crisis and the impact that it might have on their quality of life, their communities, their children's future, their retirement and society as a whole (Rooney-Browne, 2009). Under such circumstances a socially sensitive model of library management and financing is needed in order to serve the wider aims and concepts of the community at large (Sierpe, 2004). The openness of libraries, which makes them community places and sanctuaries for all, as well as their multifaceted socio-economic role, creates social capital that cannot be treated in market terms. People's trust and accountability are relevant elements in library management during the economic crisis, although, as stated by Drucker (2008), one should 'understand and apply the subject of management as an organic whole and not merely as a set of isolated elements'.

The above values and principles need to be incorporated into a 'new' library management agenda, including the following strands:

- library leadership based on long-lasting values of openness and services 'provided for all'
- libraries' social responsibility and accountability, integrating community and sustainability (e.g. environmental issues) values
- dynamic regulations for securing libraries' role and finances against threats from the consumerist forces of globalization and from market-driven economic crises
- diversification strategies through the integration and convergence of localized management of cultural heritage
- social meta-marketing to advocate and personalize library services
- innovations to improve services and the timeliness of the development of new information services
- an appreciation of the scarcity of resources, together with identification and management of various intellectual capital resources such as collective human energy, talents and creativity, as well as trust, good will, information networks etc.

Libraries stand at a crossroads of opportunity as a result of the confluence of economic and social challenges brought about by the economic recession, while (in parallel) developments in information technologies are providing a wider range of services and more channels of access to them (Kostagiolas, Margiola and Avramidou, 2011). Davis (2006) suggests switching from high-cost, market-driven library investments to a framework for fully exploring the potential of librarians' creative energies and encouraging library innovation, inclusion and people's participation. In order to increase libraries' social value and their overall socio-economic impact, library managers should assume a proactive stance and anticipate, whenever possible, the changing social and economic needs of their user communities (Kostagiolas, 2012). Indeed, social and economic development largely depends on an active, socially cohesive and well-informed population that has access to sources of information.

Conclusions, and thoughts for future research

At an international and European level, the scientific dialogue of underlying principles and 'dilemmas' has begun, and hopefully will be further developed, as a result of increasing socio-economic pressures. Indeed, the theoretical issues and the approaches that have been discussed in this chapter support the view that the scientific and social dialogue aimed at understanding the impact(s) of the economic crisis on library management must continue. Some misconceptions about public and private investments in libraries have been discussed and the need for a meta-marketing strategy for library services has been explained. The chapter has presented the management of intellectual capital as a means for a library to improve its social value and increase the level of innovation as a reactive approach. Indeed, libraries' intellectual capital, if managed properly, can improve sustainability, efficiency, effectiveness, productivity and quality (Kostagiolas, 2012).

As was noted, this chapter has aimed to increase overall awareness and knowledge of the issue by presenting a body of relevant material as a foundation for further practical and theoretical work. The chapter has certainly not aimed to address all the relevant concerns; that would be an impossible task! Indeed, the more one dwells on the relevant matters, the more practical and theoretical issues and questions are raised. Moreover, the very nature of library management suggests that the same research question can be examined from a number of different cognitive as well as interdisciplinary or even sole-disciplinary perspectives. In Greece, as in other countries badly hit by the economic crisis of 2008, neoliberal policies, 'conformist' economic efficiency criteria and 'blind', market-driven perspectives are continually reducing the number of libraries and depreciating their services. Hopefully, 'Pathos' (suffering) will become 'Mathos' (a lesson) for policy makers and library decision makers.

References

Aharony, N. (2009) Librarians' Attitudes Towards Marketing Library Services, *Journal of Librarianship and Information Science*, **41** (1), 39–50.

Asonitis, S. and Kostagiolas, P. (2010) An Analytic Hierarchy Approach for Intellectual Capital: evidence for the Greek central public libraries, *Library Management*, **31** (3), 145–161.

Broady-Preston, J. and Cox, A. (2000) The Public Library as Street Corner University: back to the future?, *New Library World*, **101** (1156), 149–60.

Buschman, J. E. (2005) *Dismantling the Public Sphere: situating and sustaining librarianship in the age of the new public philosophy*, Libraries Unlimited.

Choong, K. K. (2008) Intellectual Capital: definitions, categorization and reporting models, *Journal of Intellectual Capital*, **9** (4), 609–38.

Clarke, J. (2007) Citizen-consumers and Public Service Reform: at the limits of neoliberalism?, *Policy Futures in Education*, **5** (2), 239–48.

Davis, R. (2006) CALIMERA: mobilizing local cultural institutions for citizens, *New Library World*, **107** (1/2), 57–72.

Demoule, J.-P. (2010) The Crisis – Economic, Ideological, and Archaeological. In Schlanger, N. and Aitchison, K. (eds), *Archaeology and the Global Economic Crisis Multiple Impacts, Possible Solutions*, http://ace-archaeology.eu/ fichiers/25Archaeology-and-the-crisis.pdf.

Drucker, P. (2008) *Management, The Revised Edition*, Harper & Row.

Elsner, W. (2004) The 'New' Economy: complexity, coordination and a hybrid governance approach, *International Journal of Social Economics*, **31** (11/12), 1029–49.

Enser, P. (2001) On Continuity, Culture, Competition – Cooperation and Convergence Too, *New Library World*, **102** (1170/1171), 423–8.

Farrell, H. and Quiggin, J. (2012) *Consensus, Dissensus and Economic Ideas: the rise and fall of Keynesianism during the economic crisis*, www.henryfarrell.net/Keynes.pdf.

Ferguson, N. (2008) *The Ascent of Money: a financial history of the world*, The Penguin Press.

Gallego, I. and Rodríguez, L. (2005) Situation of Intangible Assets in Spanish Firms: an empirical analysis, *Journal of Intellectual Capital*, **6** (1), 105–26.

Germano, M. (2011) The Library Value Deficit, *The Bottom Line: Managing*

Library Finances, **24** (2), 100–6.

Goulding, A. (2006) *Public Libraries in the 21st Century: defining service and debating the future*, Ashgate.

Greene, M. and McMenemy, D. (2012) The Emergence and Impact of Neoliberal Ideology on UK Public Library Policy, 1997–2010. In Spink, A. and Heinstrom, J. (eds), *Library and Information Science Trends and Research: Europe*, Vol. 6, 13–41, Emerald Group.

Holt, G. (2007) Communicating the Value of Your Libraries, *The Bottom Line: Managing Library Finances*, **20** (3), 119–24.

Kaufmann, L. and Schneider, Y. (2004) Intangibles: a synthesis of current research, *Journal of Intellectual Capital*, **5** (3), 366–88.

Kirk, J. (1999) Information in Organisations: directions for information management, *Information Research*, **4** (3), http://informationr.net/ir/4–3/paper57.html.

Kostagiolas, P. (2012) *Managing Intellectual Capital in Libraries: beyond the balance sheet*, Chandos Publishing.

Kostagiolas, P. A. and Asonitis, S. (2009) Intangible Assets for the Academic Libraries: definitions, categorization and an exploration of management issues, *Library Management*, **30** (6/7), 419–29.

Kostagiolas, P. A. and Asonitis, S. (2011) Managing Intellectual Capital in Libraries and Information *Services*. In Woodsworth, A. (ed.), *Advances in Librarianship*, Vol. 33, Emerald Book Series.

Kostagiolas, P. A., Margiola, A. and Avramidou, A. (2011) A Library Management Response Model against the Economic Crisis: the case of public libraries in Greece, *Library Review*, **60** (6), 486–500.

Kostagiolas, P., Papadaki, E., Kanlis, G. and Papavlasopoulos, S. (2013) Responding to Crises with Alliances: evidence from an academic library survey in Greece, *Advances in Librarianship*, **36**, 247–79.

Kotler, P. (1972) *Marketing Management*, Prentice-Hall.

Kyrillidou, M. (2010) Library Value May Be Proven, if Not Self-Evident, *Research Library Issues: A Bimonthly Report from ARL, CNI, and SPARC*, **271** (August), 1–3, www.arl.org/resources/pubs/rli/archive/rli271.shtml.

Livonen, M. and Huotari, M. (2007) The University Library's Intellectual Capital, *Advances in Library Administration and Organization*, **25**, 83–96.

McMenemy, D. (2009) Rise and Demise of Neo-liberalism: TIME to reassess the impact on public libraries, *Library Review*, **58** (6), 400–4.

Missingham, R. (2005) Libraries and Economic Value: a review of recent studies, *Performance Measurements and Metrics*, **6** (3), 142–58.

Mostad-Jensen, A. (2009) The Impact of Economic Recession on Libraries: a past, present and future view, *Libreas: Library Ideas*, **5** (5), http://libreas.eu/ausgabe14/ 007mos.htm.

Musgrave, R. A. (1969) *Fiscal Systems: studies in comparative economics*, Yale University Press.

Neuhaus, C. and Snowden, K. (2003) Public Relations for a University Library: a marketing programme is born, *Library Management*, **24** (4), 193–203.

Panda, K. C. and Mandal, M. (2006) Corporate Culture in Libraries and Information Centers to Promote 'Knowledge-based Business' in IT Era, *Library Management*, **27** (6/7), 446–59.

Ramírez, Y. (2010) Intellectual Capital Models in [the] Spanish Public Sector, *Journal of Intellectual Capital*, **11** (2), 248–64.

Rooney-Browne, C. (2009) Rising to the Challenge: a look at the role of public libraries in times of recession, *Library Review*, **58** (5), 341–52.

Roos, G., Pike, S. and Fernström, L. (2005) *Managing Intellectual Capital in Practice*, Butterworth-Heinemann, Elsevier.

Samuelson, P. A. (1954) The Pure Theory of Public Expenditure, *Review of Economics and Statistics*, **36**, 387–99.

Schlanger, N. and Aitchison, K. (2010) Introduction. Archaeology and the Global Economic Crisis. In Schlanger, N. and Aitchison, K. (eds), *Archaeology and the Global Economic Crisis: multiple impacts, possible solutions*, http://ace-archaeology.eu/fichiers/25Archaeology-and-the-crisis.pdf.

Sherry, J. F. Jr (2013) Slouching Toward Utopia. In Murphy, P. E. and Sherry, J. F. Jr (eds), *Marketing and the Common Good: essays from Notre Dame on Societal Impact*, Routledge, 43–60.

Sierpe, E. (2004) Managing the Information Revolution: library management, the control of perspective technologies and the future of librarianship, *Library Management*, **25** (4/5), 177–82.

Town, J. S. (2010) Value, Impact and the Transcendent Library: progress and pressures in performance measurement and evaluation, Keynote speech, *2010 Library Assessment Conference: Building Effective, Sustainable, Practical Assessment*, Baltimore, USA.

Underwood, P. G. (1990) *Managing Change in Libraries and Information Services: a systems approach*, Clive Bingley.

Usherwood, B. (2007) *Equity and Excellence in the Public Library: why ignorance is not our heritage*, Ashgate.

Varheim, A. (2009) Public Libraries: places creating social capital?, *Library Hi Tech*, **27** (3), 372–81.

White, L. N. (2007) Unseen Measures: the need to account for intangibles, *The Bottom Line: Managing Library Finances*, **20** (2), 77–84.

Notes

1 www.maine.gov/msl/services/calculator.htm.
2 http://69.36.174.204/value-new/calculator.html.

CHAPTER 6

Introducing agile principles and management to a library organization

Daniel Forsman

Introduction

Change. The world is changing. This is not new. The human race has evolved and our societies continue to evolve and change over time, adapting to new circumstances, technologies and cultures at a rapid pace. The methods for dealing with that change in the 21st century are increasingly failing, as the people in our organizations are failing to connect their practice with the needs and vision of libraries for the future. The ways in which we operate and the structure of our work are holding back the development of libraries and the necessary change. Stephen Denning describes the need for change and how to make change happen in our emerging world:

> It's about sparking change that engages people's hearts and minds. It's about change that draws on everyone's talents and creativity, not just the schemes of a few experts at the top.
>
> Instead of articulating a top-down vision to be rolled out from above, crushing 'obstacles' in its path, it's about inviting people to dance with complexity. Instead of mining 'human resources', it's about minding the people. Instead of tending the vertical hierarchy, it's about stimulating the horizontal network. Instead of constructing firewalls to insulate the firm from its context, it's about engaging with the environment.
>
> (Denning quoted in Appelo, 2012, vii)

By introducing agile principles throughout our library organizations we are moving towards an organizational culture that can deal with change and engage and develop the services that our users love or didn't know they needed but love when they find them.

A new organization

In the spring of 2013 an organizational overhaul of Chalmers Library was announced. During the following year interviews with staff, engagement with other libraries and literature reviews commenced, leading to a new organizational structure with three departments and three cross-functional teams focused on library operations and processes (Figure 6.1).

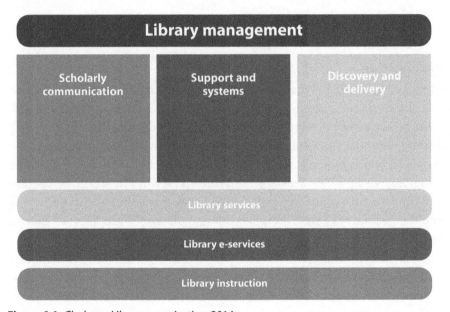

Figure 6.1 *Chalmers Library organization, 2014*

The Scholarly Communication department focuses on library services for storing, analysing, visualizing and communicating research information. It also hosts a cross-functional team working with library instruction and the information literacy programme at Chalmers.

The second department, Discovery and Delivery, focuses on acquisitions, metadata description, interlibrary loan and library systems. The department hosts a cross-functional team that works with the physical library space and the user services associated with it. The team is called Library Services.

The third department is Support and Systems. This is the department for internal library support and includes administration and finance, as well as project management, marketing and software development. This department is responsible for a cross-functional team working with the Library's web services, keeping a social media presence and organizing virtual support.

As the new organization was presented to the staff a critical question was posed from senior management. 'What is the greatest risk with this organizational change?' The answer from library staff showed great maturity, as they answered:

> The greatest risk with a change to our organization is that we will continue
> to work as previously, that the change means no change in our operations
> and that the change won't matter.

This turned management's focus from the organizational scheme to a discussion of how we conducted our work and current workflows. The new organizational scheme and structure was process oriented but it did not really influence the way in which we worked.

Drawing upon three years' experience of agile software development in the library, in which librarians had worked together with systems developers, it was decided that we would try to implement agile principles for the entire organization.

Agile

Agile means the ability to move with quick and easy grace, or to have a quick, resourceful and adaptable character (Britannica, n.d.). It has become a synonym for coping with a brisk pace of change. Used in software development, and now in other branches, agile principles are being used to create a better incentive for engagement and efficient projects. To be agile is to be able to move, adapt and constantly improve, and thus create better value for service users, according to their needs.

The Manifesto for Agile Software Development (Beck at al., 2001a) was written at a time when software developers were frustrated with the pitfalls of a waterfall methodology. It is a simple manifesto with a new set of guidelines for development focusing on working software, people and the need for change:

We are uncovering better ways of developing software by doing it and helping others do it. Through this work we have come to value:

Individuals and interactions over processes and tools
Working software over comprehensive documentation
Customer collaboration over contract negotiation
Responding to change over following a plan

That is, while there is value in the items on the right, we value the items on the left more.

(Beck et al., 2001a)

The underlying principles of the manifesto are customer satisfaction, to welcome changes (even late in a process), to do frequent updates, to collaborate and to reduce complexity by adding more perspectives. There is an emphasis on time for reflection on previous work in order to improve (Beck et al., 2001b). From these principles a number of different methodologies have evolved focusing on the different aspects of the agile principles

Speculation, development and change

Spec. Specification. Speculation. Libraries and librarians seem to be obsessed with speculation and specifications. As a profession, we are speculating about the competencies we need to develop in order to stay relevant and meaningful to our users. We speculate about user needs, library services and what we need to change. We specify and describe complex workflows, functions or processes and ask for enhancements to our domain-specific support systems, standards and protocols.

Change seems to be what is driving the obsession with speculation about the future, the next trends, and it is understandable. Since the turn of the 21st century everything has been changing. The pace of change in software development, global knowledge production and evolving user needs is staggering. However, library organizations are not built to respond to change and our greatest assets, the competencies of our work-force – our friends and colleagues – are slow to adapt to the pace of change that we see in technology and society.

We are used to thinking about problems and solutions from a speculative perspective. We investigate whether something needs to change, we describe what needs to change, the problem, the cause and the solution. Then we start working on implementing the solution after all parties have agreed on the problem and its solution. Death by committee is a common way of describing the slow pace of changing anything within our organizations. We continue to discuss and speculate instead of acting–learning–reflecting and acting again. This traditional way of developing or solving problems is very close to what is known as the waterfall development process.

The waterfall development process begins with a requirements analysis, which is followed by a series of steps where you do all of your research before you start implementing the solution. In waterfall software development the steps are usually requirements analysis, design, code, integrate, test and then deploy. In libraries we usually do the same. We do a requirements analysis, talk about the different solutions available, agree internally on how to proceed, implement a change, test it and then deploy the change – a process that can take a very long time.

Agile principles of development are a counter-reaction to the slow, waterfall methodology. Instead of speculating and specifying all eventualities, the principle is to reduce complexity by focusing on delivering value within a short time span and then to iterate the process. This is referred to as the Build–Measure–Learn feedback loop used in Lean UX.

Agile in libraries

In 1998 Lorraine Haricombe and T. J. Lusher edited *Creating the Agile Library: a management guide for librarians*. The book was an answer to meeting the rapid changes in the library environment that resulted from the impact of technology in society and higher education, an environment that had remained stable for decades. By embracing creativity, innovation and entrepreneurship, and creating an environment that encourages and supports risk taking, the agile library organization can permit the flexibility that is needed to take risks and make changes that will address users' actual needs. The book describes the concept of agility, how to prepare the organization for change by using and coping with emerging technologies. The authors of the book were forward looking and identified the rising disruption of electronic content to library services and the emerging virtual environment. The book describes the agile library from an organizational and management perspective and was well ahead of its time, urging libraries to change in order to remain relevant.

Chapter 1, 'The Agile Organization: a "better mousetrap" for libraries', introduces the concept of the agile enterprise and how to survive rapid change (from a paradigm theoretical standpoint). Chapter 6, 'Users: their impact on planning the agile library', focuses on users' needs and the changing demographics of the university. The concepts of a new learning environment, changing user needs and expectations, these ideas are well in line with the current and very modern UX (user experience) movement. If we are not adapting to changing user needs, the consequences may be dire:

> Failure to do so may render the library irrelevant.
>
> (Haricombe and Lusher, 1998, 91)

The book was well received and reviewers acknowledged the need for an 'agility of mind, innovation and public entrepreneurship' in order to cope with continual change, but by building on the core and old principles of librarianship (Hendry, 2000).

As an introduction to agile thinking, organization and management in libraries, the book is still relevant.

Roy Tennant (2001) followed up on the book's theme in a *Library Journal* article titled 'Digital Libraries – building agile organizations'. Hiring flexible staff is essential to meet the future challenges, and also to maintain organizational agility. Key factors to doing so are: communication within the organization (from below and above); encouragement by managers of individual agility in preference to standing committees; and not hiring full-time permanent staff members. These ideas are far from today's agile principles and values, where the cross-functional team is favoured over individuals and where a team learns from experience and grow together. There is less room for a single expert in the modern agile organization than in the old, specialist/functional, expert-centred organization. Also, allowing team members to grow and to learn from their mistakes is emphasized more today.

As the Library 2.0 movement talked about the need to update library services, a manifesto for librarians was defined by Laura Cohen (2006). Similar to the agile manifesto, it focuses on librarianship and the need to adapt to change and interact with users. Today the term Library 2.0 isn't being used as frequently. But the focus on user interaction and the need for valuable digital library services is. The manifesto spread out to librarians around the world, and one of its key components is about embracing change:

I will recognize that the universe of information culture is *changing fast* and that libraries need to respond positively to these changes to provide resources and services that users need and want.

(Cohen, 2006)

The manifesto still has a valid point, as librarians working in an organizational structure need to redefine the same structure that might hold them back.

Agile software development at Chalmers Library

In 2010 Chalmers Library started using an agile software development methodology called Scrum. The name comes from rugby football. A scrum is when the players huddle together. The Scrum methodology was developed during the 1990s by Jeff Sutherland and Ken Schwaber (Sutherland and Schwaber, 2013). It is an iterative and incremental methodology focusing on delivering working software with a high value for the user.

The Scrum framework has several key components and roles (Figure 6.2). Every project has a product owner. The role of the product owner is

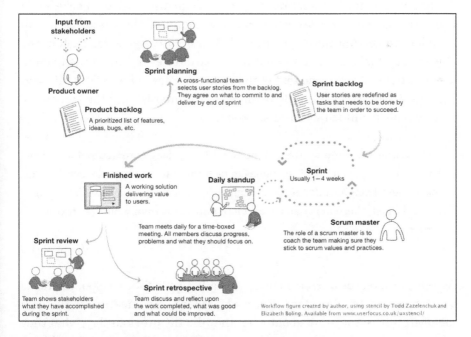

Figure 6.2 *Scrum methodology workflow*

to maintain a prioritized backlog (list) of requests for enhancements. These are usually in the form of a user story that describes what and why the user would want an enhancement or function. Anyone in the team can add stories to the backlog and these are refined as the backlog is worked on by the team. User stories can be loosely formed ideas that during refinement become detailed user stories.

Mike Cohn describes a user story like this:

> User stories are short, simple description of a feature told from the perspective of the person who desires the new capability, usually a user or customer of the system. They typically follow a simple template:
>
> As a <type of user>, I want <some goal> so that <some reason>.
>
> (Cohn, 2012)

A library-specific user story might be:

> As a librarian I would like to be able to add MARC records to the catalog so that the item will become visible in the OPAC.

At the sprint planning meeting the project team discusses the backlog and user stories. The group decides on how many of these stories it will complete in the upcoming sprint and then creates tasks for each of the stories. The tasks are usually put on a board for everyone in the team to see. But the tasks and the text of the user story are not what's of interest. It is the discussion within the team that is of interest and the stories are merely tools facilitating that discussion:

> User stories are often written on index cards or sticky notes, stored in a shoe box, and arranged on walls or tables to facilitate planning and discussion. As such, they strongly shift the focus from writing about features to discussing them. In fact, these discussions are more important than whatever text is written.
>
> (Cohn, 2012)

As work progresses during a sprint (usually two to four weeks), the tasks are completed by the team. Every day there is a meeting with team members where they talk about what they did the previous day, what they will be focusing on for the current day and whether there are any problems or obstacles. The facilitator of the daily scrum meeting is called a scrum master. The scrum master is a designated person who helps the team to follow the intentions of the methodology and facilitates and communicates with those who have an interest (stakeholders) in the team's work and progress.

At the end of a sprint there is sprint review where the team demonstrates its work for stakeholders and gets feedback on its work. As a part of the review there is a feedback session with just the team, focusing on the relations, problems and possibilities during the sprint.

The process then restarts and the team selects new user stories to work on for the upcoming sprint.

Scrum is a controlled methodology with a focus on the rapid delivery of working software. By reducing complexity and focusing the work on specific aspects, the team can respond fast to changes in requirements. This also forces the team members to work together and to talk about what they are doing (or not doing). Any problems are identified early and can't be hidden away.

Cross-functional teams

As the software development team at Chalmers Library worked with different library-oriented projects the team became more cross-functional. Instead of having librarians as stakeholders in a project it started to include them in the development team. This led to a mutual development and understanding of the library business between the developers and librarians, who started to share knowledge and train each other.

Gary Chin describes the cross-functional team and members' roles as

> defined by expertise and a desire for team success, while a classic team is
> defined by title and function. In a team defined by title and function there are
> barriers and boundaries between team members. In an agile team roles are
> changed, swapped and some even eliminated as the team work together to
> overcome and solve the problems they face.
>
> (Chin, 2004)

Management and agile

After running several projects using cross-functional teams of librarians and developers, senior management at Chalmers Library started discussing how to implement agile principles in the entire organization. Traditional business management can be a severe threat to agile methodology. It is important for managers to trust the agile team and not to micro-manage its work. It is not the role of the manager to tell the team how to solve a problem. That responsibility lies with the team. The manager is supposed to help the team and to remove obstacles, allowing it to focus on tasks.

The team is supposed to be self-organizing and to take responsibility. There is no project leader in a traditional sense; instead, the members of the group communicate and agree upon actions in order to solve the tasks in a sprint.

Managers are still important as stakeholders, and by communicating with the product owner they can help to prioritize the backlog and add user stories. By introducing agile principles, senior management has to change and move towards what Peter Saddington (2013) describes as the 'servant leadership', where the most important job of a team leader or a manager is to remove obstacles or to resolve dependencies between team members and teams, to remind the team of the mission/value of the project and to protect the team and filter non-essential information and meetings.

Understanding your context: user experience and design

As Chalmers Library services became more electronic a divide between the physical library and the electronic library appeared. Researchers no longer had to visit the library in order to access information. Both they and our students can access our information services at any time, from anywhere. The people whom librarians meet in the physical library are a minority of those who use our services. Designing library services based upon interactions with that minority will not develop the services that the majority of our users need. Trusting a librarian's appraisal of user needs based upon the experience of dealing with only a minority of our users is dangerous and an incorrect representation of the user community and its needs. Electronic resources and services have created a gap between the majority of our users and the people who work in the library. In order to develop the library, we need to update our impressions of what our users are doing and what they need and do not need.

By turning to the growing discipline of user-centred design, interaction design and UX, we can access tools that can be used to close the knowledge gap between the library and its users.

First of all, libraries are not in a position to influence or change user groups' behaviour. We can reach out to, enlighten and change individuals by reference or library instruction. But it is extremely difficult to influence or change a group's behaviour. Libraries either can continue to bang their heads against a wall as they try to enlighten their users about the benefits of their services, or they can learn more about groups' behaviours and design services that fit those behaviours. By adapting services to user behaviour, we may get users to see their value and to use our services.

Our value lies in making the lives of our users easier. Without excessive marketing, we can do that without telling them that we are doing it. There is reward enough in focusing on doing the right things and doing them well. We will be acknowledged in this way.

Get out of the building

Since the majority of users are not located within the walls of the library it is crucial that the library go out of the building to meet and learn about its users in their own environment. By performing user interviews, using open questions and asking users to describe what they are doing in their interaction with the library and to tell us how they study or conduct their research, so patterns of user behaviour will emerge. By grouping patterns of user behaviour, libraries can create specific personas to represent user behaviours. Nielsen defined persona as follows:

> A persona is not the same as an archetype or a person. As it has been described,
>
> > the special aspect of a persona description is that you do not look at the entire person but use the focus area as a lens to highlight the relevant attitudes and the specific context associated with these.
>
> (Nielsen, 2013, 7)

Personas are based upon actual user behaviour, but are not real people.

A persona is based upon behaviour, and not upon opinions about behaviour held by librarians or other stakeholders. Meet David, one of Chalmers Library's three personas used for developing a new website

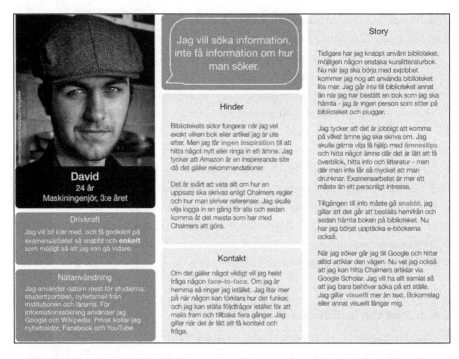

Figure 6.3 *David, one of three personas used by Chalmers Library during the redesign of library web pages*

(Figure 6.3) (Olofsson, 2012). The persona description tells us about David so that we can connect. He has a name, age and profile. The profile tells us about how he is using the internet, what motivates him, obstacles, how he prefers to interact with the library and a story describing his situation as he searches for information. The persona is illustrated with a quote from an actual user interview.

By focusing on what the users are doing, and not focusing on what the users say that they are doing, libraries can avoid making design mistakes. It is common user behaviour either to try to please the interviewers or to be too critical. As the interview results are being processed, the focus should be not on what the user said they where doing, but on the behaviour of the user. In user-centred design there is a famous cartoon showcasing different perspectives on what a product should look like. Different professional roles describe what they think a swing should look like and what the customer needs. But in the end what the customer really needed was a very simple solution (CartouCHe, 2012).

When we interview users it is important to keep in mind that they are not tasked to solve the library's problems. It would be equally wrong to ask the librarians to solve those problems on the basis of their own opinions:

> One of the worst ways of approaching design is to let the customers do it. Customers are good at pointing out a need, a pain point in the market, but they are lousy at solving the problem.
>
> (Werby, 2011)

If you ask the users what they want and how they want to solve a problem you will end up with specific and detailed needs. Another famous example of this is when Homer Simpson designs a car in the episode 'Oh Brother, Where Art Thou?' in the TV series *The Simpsons*. The car Homer designs is everything he wants, but unfortunately for the car maker the design is so Homer-specific that no one else is interested in buying it and the factory goes bankrupt (Oh Brother, Where Art Thou?, 2014)

It is important for libraries to get out of the building and to engage with their users on what they are doing. By focusing on what users are doing, on their context and not on what they are saying that they need, we will receive data that can feed into the design of services adapted to users' needs and behaviour, services that will fit with usage patterns and that are natural and intuitive.

As the context of our library is changing, there are some questions that we need to ask again and again for each project or strategic plan.

Who are the people we are designing for? What is the activity (or activities) that they are trying to do? And what are the contexts in which they are trying to operate (Anderson, 2009)?

Conclusion: moving forward

Chalmers Library is still exploring the possibilities and challenges of working with agile development and management. It is an iterative and evolving process but the benefits far outweigh the drawbacks, as the organization can learn and respond to change, reprioritize how resources are allocated, avoid knowledge silos, build strong teams and identify uncertainties early.

As the library organization at Chalmers continues to evolve and in our efforts to offer services of real value to students and researchers, agile principles are slowly finding their way into the core values of operations. Scrum is now just one of the methods being used as library staff explore Lean UX, Kanban, Scrum-ban, how to use value curves, impact maps and creating 'minimum viable' products to gain as much information as possible about user acceptance.

Introducing agile principles into the library has sparked a heated debate among staff on what we do and why. Agile methods expose values and highlight differences in opinion and so it takes a mature group of staff to work with them. But if they are successful, the library can adapt and respond to changes and deliver services of high value to its users.

The stages described in this chapter are nothing but baby steps, as we feel our way forward.

Acknowledgements

This article is the result of iterative work at Chalmers Library and could not have been completed without the support of all library staff. In our efforts to explore, adapt and evolve library services using agile principles, I thank you all.

References

Anderson, S. P. (2009) Fundamentals of Experience Design. Retrieved from www.poetpainter.com/thoughts/article/ia-summit-2009-the-fundamentals-of-experience-design.

Appelo, J. (2012) *How to Change the World*, Jojo Ventures Bv.

Beck, K. et al. (2001a) Manifesto for Agile Software Development, http://agilemanifesto.org/.

Beck, K. et al. (2001b) Principles behind the Agile Manifesto, http://agilemanifesto.org/principles.html.

Britannica (n.d.) Britannica Academic Edition – Dictionary, www.britannica.com/dictionary/agile.

CartouCHe (2012) User Centered Design, www.e-cartouche.ch/content_reg/cartouche/ui_access/en/html/GUIDesign_UCD.html.

Chin, G. (2004) *Agile Project Management: how to succeed in the face of changing project requirements*, AMACOM.

Cohen, L. (2006) A Librarian's 2.0 Manifesto, https://web.archive.org/web/20070209003635/http://liblogs.albany.edu/library

20/2006/11/a_librarians_20_manifesto.html.

Cohn, M. (2012) User Stories, www.mountaingoatsoftware.com/agile/user-stories.

Haricombe, L. J. and Lusher, T. J. (1998) *Creating the Agile Library: a management guide for librarians*, Greenwood.

Hendry, J. D. (2000) Creating the Agile Library: a management guide for librarians, *Library Review*, **49** (1), 40–8.

Nielsen, L. (2013) *Personas – user focused design*, Springer.

Oh Brother, Where Art Thou? (2014) Wikipedia, http://en.wikipedia.org/wiki/Oh_Brother,_Where_Art_Thou%3F.

Olofsson, K. (2012) Vi presenterar våra tre personor Sofia, David och Maria, http://blog.lib.chalmers.se/2012/05/14/vi-presenterar-vara-tre-personor-sofia-david-och-maria/.

Saddington, P. (2013) *The Agile Pocket Guide: a quick start to making your business agile using Scrum and beyond*, John Wiley & Sons.

Sutherland, J. and Schwaber, K. (2013) The Scrum Guide – The Definitive Guide to Scrum: the rules of the game, https://www.scrum.org/Portals/0/Documents/Scrum%20Guides/2013/Scrum-Guide.pdf.

Tennant, R. (2001) Digital Libraries – building agile organizations, *Library Journal*, **126** (7), 30.

Werby, O. (2011) Entropy and Design, www.interfaces.com/blog/2011/04/entropy-design.

CHAPTER 7

The role of professional associations in changing times

Susan Henczel

Introduction

This book covers many of the aspects of change that are influencing the nature of the profession of librarianship. One of the key insights that emerges when these aspects are put together in this way is that, although technological developments form the basis of change in the profession in terms of processes and perceptions, it is time to focus on the people aspect if the profession is to be sustained and valued by society.

Like many other professions, librarians have faced new ways of working as organizations and institutions have sought efficiencies and quality improvements through technological solutions. At the same time, they have experienced changes in the way the profession is valued by organizations and, more widely, as technologies enable user-initiated solutions to information needs. The declining perception of the value of librarians in education, business and the community has been the basis of decisions to close libraries and deprofessionalize workforces, despite studies that have attempted to prove value in these areas.

Professional associations have a primary responsibility to represent the profession they were established to support. The national associations often have a responsibility to work with educators, employers, legislators, funding bodies and other professional bodies that have influence on the profession. National associations vary in how they see their responsibilities to the profession. Some focus on the people within the profession, while others focus on the libraries and other employing institutions. Some focus on both of these areas equally. Some embrace emerging fields and non-traditional roles more readily than others. Many invite different groups such as educators and paraprofessionals to take up association membership. These variations have altered the membership characteristics and structures of many national associations, and on an international level have contributed to inconsistency in what can be expected from a national library association.

The changes that the profession has undergone since the mid-1980s have consequences for all library associations, and in particular for national library associations. The core roles and responsibilities that we place on the national associations have not changed, and so we can expect them to be concerned about education, research, advocacy, training and development, communication, regulation, standards and legislation. We can also expect them to consider the professional identity that they help to shape in their members and how that plays out in terms of their professionalism within both the profession and the workplace. The challenges resulting from generational issues, including declining membership numbers and reduced participation by members in association activities, have forced many associations to consider their future business models and, in particular, how they recruit and retain members, what activities they should engage in and what products and services they should provide.

The challenges facing library associations are those that are being faced by professional associations globally across a diverse range of professions and are not unique to the profession of librarianship and information management (Sladek, 2011).

A changing professional environment

There are three aspects of the changing professional environment that have direct consequences for professional associations. These are (1) professional territory and boundaries, (2) demographics and (3) perception of value.

Professional territory and boundaries

As the roles of librarians have broadened, the profession has become more complex through convergence with other fields and disciplines, including information and/or communications technology, information systems, content management, web design and development, information architecture, records management and knowledge management (Wilson and Halpin, 2006).

Many librarians are now working outside the traditional library structure, with academic librarians likely to be working within faculties, research groups or project teams within the broader university environment. Similarly for special librarians, the closure and/or downsizing of many of our corporate, government and other special libraries has seen the professionals become embedded into operational and/or strategic units within the organization. More and more public librarians are likely to be working with their community groups and providing outreach services outside their libraries. The consequences of these changes include the fact that the professional territory and boundaries of librarianship have become increasingly unclear as those working outside libraries encroach on, and merge with, areas that either did not exist previously or have traditionally belonged to other fields, disciplines or professions.

Many might argue that the unique professional body of knowledge (PBOK) associated with the profession of librarianship exists and is alive and well. However, others would disagree. As well as struggling with the identification and articulation of the PBOK associated with their profession, many librarians are experiencing tension between loyalty to their profession and loyalty to their employing organization (Noordegraaf, 2011b). As more librarians work outside a physical library structure the likelihood of their becoming more loyal to their organization than to their profession increases. This also leads to an increase in networking and communication outside the profession, which may detract from the networking and communication librarians engage in within the profession. While 'association' is still important to individuals, new ways of communicating, including through social media, provide flexible ways of connecting and communicating and enable members to associate without the need for formal associations.

Each of these elements influences the professional identity held by the individual members of the profession, and, in turn, their professionalism, in the way they behave in the workplace and as a member of their profession in terms of commitment and professional participation (Henczel and Macauley, 2013).

Demographics

In addition to the changes in the environment in which the profession of librarianship operates, the demographics within the profession have also changed. 'Generational issues' are seen by many as a key trend that will shape the future of associations (Gunn, 2002). Like many professions, librarianship is an ageing one, with many of its members facing retirement. As the baby boomers, who make up the largest proportion of association membership, move into retirement there may not be sufficient younger members, Gen Y, X or Millennials, to take their places. This presents a number of challenges for associations, including the need to leverage their members' knowledge and expertise before they retire, and the management of members in their pre-retirement years, particularly in terms of maintaining their interest and commitment to their work. It also influences the business models that they choose to adopt, how they physically structure themselves and how they market to, and communicate with, their members.

In addition to generational issues, the profession is changing in how it identifies the work to be done with the skills required. Today we see the more traditional roles often being delegated to support staff (Davis and Spalding, 2005), while the professionals take on wider roles related to technology, contracts, learning support and events management (Australian Library and Information Association, n.d.). As well as integrating members from various generations in our workplaces, we are also often integrating librarians and non-librarians, who are often doing similar work. This, combined with the fact that many librarians are working outside physical libraries, or choosing to use their skills in careers other than librarianship, changes the skill-sets that are required for career success and influences outsiders' perception of the profession.

Perception of the profession

Librarianship is a profession, distinct from the libraries in which many members of the profession are employed. Despite this, as the profession evolves it continues to be influenced by the value perceptions associated with libraries, as well as by those associated with the profession of librarianship. As value perceptions regarding libraries and librarians within organizations have evolved we have experienced declining budgets, library closures and the decentralized redeployment of librarianship expertise throughout organizations and institutions (Financial Times Corporate, 2013). In the special library environment, employers see librarians as a part of the libraries that they no longer have. As corporate and government libraries have disappeared, so have the staff attached to them, except where employers have recognized the value of the professional expertise and redeployed it where needed within the organization.

Declining budgets have meant library closures across all library sectors, and where the libraries have been 'saved', work-forces are often reduced and deprofessionalized through the use of unqualified, lesser-qualified or volunteer staff. The value placed on the profession is formed by what people see and experience, and increasingly, particularly in public libraries, their interactions are with customer-service staff rather than with the professionals. The expertise is largely hidden behind the scenes and is invisible to the library users. This is also the case in academic library services, where information is provided to students through learning management systems and other academic teaching channels and where its library origins are not evident.

As user-initiated information solutions become the norm for access to both personal and professional information, the role of the librarian becomes increasingly invisible, and so it becomes increasingly important to identify the librarian's work and the role played in providing information solutions, regardless of the purpose or sector. As a profession, librarians understand what difference they can make to education, business and communities – but they often struggle to articulate this to others. This inability to articulate their contribution to information solutions is often exacerbated by the terminology that has evolved in line with the changes in value perceptions. Some feel that the move away from the terms 'librarian' and 'librarianship' in favour of 'information management' in our library schools and workplaces has confused the profession with the job roles. The emerging job titles that attempt to reconcile new and old are often seen as awkward and/or meaningless in professional terms (Davis, 2008), while some agree that the terminology may become sector specific, with 'librarian' being used in public libraries and 'information professional' being seen as more strategic and being adopted in special libraries (Australian Library and Information Association, 2014). Regardless of the views of individuals about what the profession should be called, this influences views about what the associations should be called and causes rifts within the profession and within the association memberships.

Professional associations

A professional association is a body of persons engaged in the same profession, formed usually to control entry into the profession, maintain standards and represent the profession in discussions with other bodies (Noordegraaf, 2011a). The works of Hall (1968) and Wilensky (1964) tell us that the establishment of a professional association is a core component in a field of work's becoming known as a profession and also a core element in the development of professional identity (how we feel about being a member of a particular profession) and professionalism (how we behave as a member of a particular profession).

As a profession changes and evolves, so must the professional associations that support it. It is the professional association that sets out the 'body of knowledge, skills, competencies and shared or core values' for the profession, and each of these components must remain aligned with the profession. 'The core values of a profession are set out by the professional associations through which practitioners become registered or accredited' (Davis, 2008, 70). Close bonds are needed between the members of a changing profession and their association, so that they change in line with one another (Watson, 2002). Noordegraaf's works on the relationship between the changing organizational requirements of professions and the resulting changes in what people need from their professional associations suggests that 'professional associations, as non-organizing forms of social organizing, are crucial for construing and organizing members. They create and symbolize professional behaviours and practices. They bring together professional workers, define professional work, establish boundaries and demarcate fields, standardize work methods and form professional loyalties' (Noordegraaf, 2011a, 468).

Library associations

The library and information profession is supported by a diverse range of professional associations, each providing support services and resources for members of the profession. The general categorization of library associations is international, national, regional, state and local (Ghosh, 2006). At each of these levels there are associations that support library workers in all sectors, as well as others that are sector or discipline specific.

National library associations

Most countries have a national library association and many have more than one. National associations such as the Australian Library and Information Association (ALIA), the American Library Association (ALA), the Library and Information Association of New Zealand Aotearoa (LIANZA) and the UK's Chartered Institute of Library and Information Professionals (CILIP) support libraries across all sectors, including academic, special, school and public. Most national associations are accrediting bodies for the library and information science curricula provided by the tertiary sector in their respective countries. Today's figures indicate that membership of the national associations is not only declining but is also a relatively small proportion of potential membership.

Core roles and responsibilities of national library associations

A scan of the existing literature about library associations provides insight into the core roles and responsibilities that we can expect from a national association:

1   *Education*: the accreditation of LIS programmes to ensure that they reflect the core practices and respond to the emerging needs of the profession (Broady-Preston, 2010; Haycock, 2007; Lynch, 2010; Partridge and Yates, 2012; I. Thomas et al., 2012).
2   *Research*: the development and communication of research agendas, and the effective communication of research outputs; this provides a bridge between research and practice (Fisher, 1997; Haddow, 2010; McKnight and Hagy, 2009).
3   *Advocacy*: ensuring that political leaders and funders at all levels of government understand the role of libraries and the profession in their communities and organizations and in government itself (American Society of Association Executives, 2012); ensuring that communities understand how libraries can support education, literacy, community development and engagement and social inclusion (Borges, 2005); ensuring that organizations understand the role and value of the profession (Noordegraaf, 2011b).
4   *Professional updating*: the provision of relevant continuing professional development (CPD) and training opportunities and the communication of industry issues and developments (Abram, 2006;

Barry and Garcia-Febo, 2012; Broady-Preston and Cossham, 2011; Janosik, Carpenter and Creamer, 2006; Milton, 2003; Rusaw, 1995; Thomas, Satpathi and Satpathi, 2010).

5 *Communication*: establishing communication channels to connect people geographically and within and across disciplines (Abram, 2006; Bennett, 2011).

6 *Industry*: monitoring recruitment, employment levels, conditions and opportunities (Clift, 1963).

7 *Professionalism and professional identity*: ensuring that the profession is positioned appropriately and well regarded, from both the inside and the outside (Broady-Preston, 2010; Evetts, 2003; Karseth and Nerland, 2007; McGuigan, 2011; Noordegraaf, 2011a; Wilson and Halpin, 2006).

8 *Contribution to the information society*: creating policy frameworks in 'an environment of information-intensive organizations, effective information sectors, widespread social use of information and a pervasive system of lifelong learning' (Moore, 2001, 172).

9 *Regulation, standards and legislation*: the development of standards, charters and guidelines and contribution to regional and national legislation such as on copyright and intellectual property (Ammons, 1994; Cooke, 1975; Fang, 1979; Poll, 2006; Quinn and McCallum, 2011; Zaiane, 2011; Zverevich, 1992).

10 *Leadership*: leadership of and for the profession, as inherent in all of the above; the associations also have a role in developing leaders within the profession (Ammons-Stephens et al., 2009; Clift, 1963; Dick, 2012; Glendenning and Gordon, 1997; Woolls, 2009).

As associations address these roles and responsibilities with varying levels of success, their futures lie in how they deal with today's needs and expectations and the strategies they develop to sustain them (Lachance, 2006).

The implications of the changing environment for national library associations

National library associations have a long history, with most close to or having already reached their centenary. Technological developments, however, from information and communication technologies (ICT) to publishing, have changed and continue to change the environment that they were established to support. Consequently, relevant support mechanisms for members of the profession come in the form of informal networks, non-library groups and associations, subject- or discipline-specific associations and networks, often to the detriment of the national library association.

While the core roles and responsibilities remain the same as they have been for decades, many professionals are citing the irrelevance of the association as one of their reasons for not joining (Dalton and Digman, 2007). This suggests there is a disconnect between the association and the professional work that people are doing. The emergence of smaller groups within the professional association environment is often a result of the perceived irrelevance of the national association, as members 'splinter into sub-units or completely separate associations' (Davis and Spalding, 2005, 167). The fragmentation caused by the emergence of smaller groups impacts not only on the national association in terms of diversity but also on the profession itself, as there is no longer a unified, single voice. The national associations have shifted from being a primary 'umbrella' association supporting a profession in a specific country or region to being just one of many that members can choose to join. In attempting to redefine themselves, some have retained their professional association focus, others have become membership organizations and some have claimed elements of both so as to become hybrid associations (Coerver and Byers, 2011).

Declining membership

Membership of national library associations is declining, due to factors such as shrinking financial support from employers, greater demands on professionals' time, the presence of a broad choice of seemingly more relevant associations, including those established to support non-library professions, the cost of membership and/or a perceived lack of value for money (Richards, 2002), irrelevance and competition from other associations (Dalton and Digman, 2007) and the retirement of the baby boomers (Davis and Spalding, 2005). It has been suggested anecdotally that there is a lack of interest on the part of younger professionals in joining the national associations. The emergence of strong and active new graduates' groups seems to contradict this, while confirming the findings of those studying generational issues who say that the younger generations are just as likely to engage with associations, but maybe not in the same ways as previous generations (Brooks, 2006). Additionally, as membership of professional library associations is voluntary, the various levels and types of associations are competing with one another for members. Where previous generations may have chosen the national association for altruistic reasons, younger generations are faced with a multitude of choices ranging from local, regional, state, national and international to those specializing in specific subjects or disciplines.

Declining membership of national associations has significant consequences:

For education and research: There are implications for the associations, as the accrediting bodies for the LIS profession, in terms of the quality and relevance of both professional education and research, due to a disconnect between the profession and those accrediting the courses and conducting research.

For advocacy and lobbying: Reduced numbers lessen the associations' ability to influence political agendas and funding arguments.

For the sustainability of the association: The associations require membership fees and monies from the sale of products and services in order to operate. Declining revenues now and known revenues in the future influence the associations' ability to plan strategically and to ensure sustainability.

For the sustainability of the profession: Being less than representative of the profession makes it more difficult to manage and monitor the professional territory, boundaries and status of the profession.

Declining participation levels

Today's library associations rely on an active membership to develop and deliver their products and services. For the associations as largely volunteer organizations, activity in the form of engagement, commitment and participation on behalf of members will determine what products and services they can provide, how well they can engage in advocacy and lobbying activities and attract lucrative partnerships, and the types of opportunities they can provide to their members through committee, board and working group involvement. Professionals are increasingly time poor and unlikely to volunteer their time and expertise unless they see a personal or professional benefit. This was particularly true of the baby boomer generation, which currently makes up the largest proportion of members. Predictions for the participation levels of Gen X and Y in the years to come do not necessarily indicate a decline but, rather, a change in the type and length of participation (Brooks, 2006). These issues are testing the operating models of our national associations in terms of their funding and resourcing.

Emerging opportunities for national library associations

Changes in the profession of librarianship present the national library associations with a number of emerging opportunities not only to ensure their survival and sustainability but to enable them to redefine their role in supporting the profession. This can be done by focusing on demonstrating the value of the profession, defining territories and boundaries, reducing fragmentation, understanding the demographic characteristics and leveraging them, and clarifying the role of the profession so that it can be understood by society. Understanding that there are also intangibles involved is also important, as members talk about having a sense of belonging and a feeling of connectedness that result in knowledge, skills attitudes and behaviours that contribute to their career success.

Demonstration of value

Articulation and demonstration of the value that the profession can bring to education, business and the community goes beyond economic value, to include impact assessment, i.e. the difference that the utilization of professional skills and knowledge makes to the institution, organization or community. The use of formal impact assessment standards and frameworks will ensure methodological consistency to facilitate comparisons.

Professional territory and boundaries

Convergence and the emergence of new roles have blurred the boundaries of the profession in relation to others such as information technology, knowledge management and information systems. It has become increasingly important to stake out the territory that the profession of librarianship wishes to claim and to define and describe the unique PBOK that librarianship encompasses. This will involve clearly defining boundaries and articulating the role of the librarian within those boundaries and will enable other professions to understand not only what librarians do, but also how to use them to add value to the work of other professions.

Unification

By addressing the current fragmentation of the profession, national associations will improve the cohesiveness of the professional community, which will, in turn, improve information dissemination and communication within the profession. It will facilitate the development and application of standards and guidelines across sectors and enable them to be promulgated across the entire profession and not just to national association members. By embracing smaller groups and bringing them under the 'umbrella' of the national association, the single voice representing the profession becomes stronger and the support provided is more pervasive.

Demographics

In an ageing profession such as librarianship it is important to leverage the knowledge and expertise of members prior to their retirement. Associations have the opportunity to connect with members through their fellows' groups and groups established for retired members. Other opportunities include the development of programmes that address the integration of multiple generations in workplaces and in the profession. Shifting demographics also provide opportunities to explore new ways of engaging younger generations who may question the value that they receive in return for their membership fees and who are faced with many options in the competitive association environment (Brooks, 2006).

Partnerships and collaboration

Professional associations overall are forming relationships with other associations and with institutions such as universities (Beaton, 2014).

Within the library and information sector 'collaborative bridges among library associations and across international borders are being formed' (Davis and Spalding, 2005, 165) to provide educational programmes, events and services. These include creative partnerships between associations and library schools, research groups and project teams in industry.

International consistency

International consistency in all aspects of the profession has the potential to contribute to the overall understanding of the profession, impacting on the status of the profession, the value perceptions of employers and communities, and librarianship's relationship to other professions. Consistency in things such as qualifications and the standards and guidelines under which professionals operate is important, as is international acceptance of professional terminology, definitions and descriptions, and the nomenclature related to job titles. This would facilitate global comparisons and employment mobility (Broady-Preston, 2010; Manpower Group, 2011).

Intangibles

Members of national library associations cite intangibles as one of their primary reasons for retaining membership (Henczel, 2014). These intangibles include a 'sense of belonging' and a 'feeling of connectedness' to others. Intangibles such as these influence not only which association a person chooses to join, but how long they retain their membership and how much they participate in association activities. Leveraging these intangibles provides a potential benefit for both the association and the profession as members report increased self-confidence in the workplace and in their career management, higher levels of empowerment and better decision making.

Conclusion

Many professions are undergoing change as a result of advances in technology, changing demographics and shifting value perceptions. Librarianship is no exception. The changes experienced by a profession have direct consequences for the professional associations that support it, particularly the national 'umbrella' associations that influence formal education and research, engage in advocacy and lobbying, provide CPD, and promote communication within the profession – and about the role and value of the profession to those outside it.

The consequences of these changes include declining membership, and lower levels of participation by those who do choose to join. These are primarily attributed to the cost of membership, the relevance of the association to the work that people are doing in their workplaces and competition, in that there are many associations and groups that people can join that may be more relevant to their work than the national association. The decline in membership of the national associations has far-reaching effects, including consequences for education and research, for advocacy and lobbying, and for the sustainability of the profession and the associations themselves.

The consequences of these changes also bring opportunities for the associations to strengthen their roles if they can effectively demonstrate the value of the profession to communities, education and industry; establish and articulate professional boundaries and territories; unify the profession so as to reduce and, ideally, eliminate fragmentation; address the challenges resulting from shifting demographics; develop partnerships and collaborative arrangements with other associations so as to reduce competition and increase international consistency to support the mobility of the profession; and understand the intangibles that influence people to join and retain their membership of associations.

References

Abram, S. (2006) Technoschism: the real world and libraries, librarians and our associations: a view from Canada, *Library Management*, **27** (1/2), 14–25.

American Society of Association Executives (2012) The Value and Purpose of Association Lobbying, ASAE.

Ammons, D. N. (1994) The Role of Professional Associations in Establishing and Promoting Performance Standards for Local Government, *Public Productivity and Management Review*, **17** (3), 281–98.

Ammons-Stephens, S., Cole, H. J., Jenkins-Gibbs, K., Richie, C. F. and Weare, W. H. Jr (2009) Developing Core Leadership Competencies for the Library Profession, *Library Leadership and Management*, **23** (2), 63–74.

Australian Library and Information Association (n.d.) About the Profession, https://www.alia.org.au/information-and-resources/about-sector.

Australian Library and Information Association (2014) *Future of the Library and Information Science Profession*, ALIA.

Barry, T. and Garcia-Febo, L. (2012) Expanding Horizons – developing the next generation of international professionals, *Australian Library Journal*, **61** (1), 16–21.

Beaton, G. (2014) *2014 Associations Roundtable*, Beaton Research and Consulting.

Bennett, M. H. (2011) The Benefits of Non-library Professional Organization Membership for Liaison Librarians, *Journal of Academic Librarianship*, **37** (1), 46–53.

Borges, M. (2005) Library Advocacy Starts at Home, *The Bottom Line: Managing Library Finances*, **18** (3), 110–11.

Broady-Preston, J. (2010) The Information Professional of the Future: polymath or dinosaur? *Library Management*, **31** (1/2), 66–78.

Broady-Preston, J. and Cossham, A. (2011) Keeping the Information Profession Up To Date: are compulsory schemes the answer?, *IFLA Journal*, **37**, 28–38.

Brooks, A. C. (2006) *Generations and the Future of Association Participation: report to The William E. Smith Institute for Association Research*, The William E. Smith Institute for Association Research.

Clift, D. H. (1963) The Role of Library Associations: a symposium: the Association's viewpoint, *Bulletin of the Medical Library Association*, **51** (1), 44–9.

Coerver, H. and Byers, M. (2011) *Race for Relevance: 5 radical changes for associations*, ASAE: The Center for Association Leadership.

Cooke, E. D. (1975) The Role of ALA and Other Library Associations in the Promotion of Library Legislation, *Library Trends*, **24** (1), 137–53.

Dalton, J. and Digman, M. (2007) *The Decision to Join: how individuals determine value and why they choose to belong*, ASAE and The Center for Association Leadership.

Davis, C. (2008) Librarianship in the 21st Century – crisis or transformation? *Public Library Quarterly*, **27** (1), 57–82.

Davis, M. E. K. and Spalding, H. H. (2005) Changing Roles for Library Associations. In Cleyle, S. E. and McGillis, L. M. (eds), *Last One Out Turn Off the Lights*, Scarecrow Press.

Dick, A. L. (2012) Library Associations: a leadership role?, *Information Development*, **28** (1), 11–12.

Evetts, J. (2003) The Sociological Analysis of Professionalism: occupational change in the modern world, *International Sociology*, **18** (2), 395–415.

Fang, J. R. (1979) National Library Associations and Their Impact on Library Legislation: an international survey, *IFLA Journal*, **5** (4), 276–81.

Financial Times Corporate (2013) The Evolving Value of Information Management and the Five Essential Attributes of the Modern Information Professional, www.sla.org/wp-content/uploads/2014/03/FT-SLA-Report.pdf.

Fisher, W. (1997) The Value of Professional Associations, *Library Trends*, **46**, 320–30.

Ghosh, M. (2006) The Emerging Role of National and Regional Associations in Library Development: an Indian perspective, *Library Review*, **55** (1), 45–58.

Glendenning, B. J. and Gordon, J. C. (1997) Professional Associations: promoting leadership in a career, *Library Trends*, **46**, 258–77.

Gunn, J. (2002) Generational Marketing, www.csae.com/Resources/ArticlesTools/View/ArticleId/1507/Generational-Marketing.

Haddow, G. (2010) Communicating Research to Practice: the role of professional association publications, *Library and Information Research*, **34** (108), 33–44.

Hall, R. H. (1968) Professionalism and Bureaucratization, *American Sociological Review*, **33** (1), 92–104.

Haycock, K. (2007) Education for Library and Information Studies in Canada: a cross-cultural comparison, *New Library World*, **108** (1–2), 32–9.

Henczel, S. (2014) Professional Associations as Catalysts for Change through Leadership and Consolidation, paper presented at the SLA 2014, Vancouver, BC, Canada.

Henczel, S. and Macauley, P. (2013) Professionalism: exploring the role and responsibility of professional associations, paper presented at the LIANZA 2013, Hamilton, New Zealand.

Janosik, S. M., Carpenter, S. and Creamer, D. G. (2006) Beyond Professional Preparation Programs: the role of professional associations in ensuring a high quality workforce, *College Student Affairs Journal*, **25** (2), 228–37.

Karseth, B., and Nerland, M. (2007) Building Professionalism in a Knowledge Society: examining discourses of knowledge in four professional associations, *Journal of Education and Work*, **20** (4), 335–55.

Lachance, J. R. (2006) Learning, Community give Library and Information Associations a Bright Future, *Library Management*, **27** (1/2), 6–13.

Lynch, B. P. (2010) Professional Associations and Library Education, *RBM: A Journal of Rare Books, Manuscripts and Cultural Heritage*, **11** (1), 32–46.

Manpower Group (2011) *Entering the Human Age: thought leadership insights*, Manpower Group.

McGuigan, G. S. (2011) Crisis of Professionalism in Public Services: addressing challenges to librarianship from a public administration perspective, *Library Review*, **60** (7), 560–74.

McKnight, M. and Hagy, C. R. (2009) The Research Imperative: Medical Library Association policy and the curricula of schools of library and information science, *Journal of the Medical Library Association*, **97** (2), 134–6.

Milton, J. (2003) Professional Associations as Learning Systems: learning + strategy + action = strategic learning, *Advances in Developing Human Resources*, **5**, 173–81.

Moore, N. (2001) Library Associations: their role in supporting the creation of information societies, *IFLA Journal*, **27** (3), 171–5.

Noordegraaf, M. (2011a) Remaking Professionals? How associations and professional education connect professionalism and organizations, *Current Sociology*, **59**, 465–88.

Noordegraaf, M. (2011b) Risky Business: how professionals and professional fields (must) deal with organizational issues, *Organization Studies*, **32**, 1349–71.

Partridge, H. and Yates, C. (2012) A Framework for the Education of the Information Professions in Australia, *The Australian Library Journal*, **61** (2), 81–94.

Poll, R. (2006) Standardized Measures in the Changing Information Environment, *Performance Measurement and Metrics*, **7** (3), 127–41.

Quinn, S. and McCallum, I. (2011) Continuous Improvement: national standards and guidelines for Australia's public libraries, *Australasian Public Libraries and Information Services*, **24** (3), 101–6.

Richards, G. (2002) Why Do Librarians Join Library Associations, or Do They?, *New Zealand Libraries*, **49** (6), 199–207.

Rusaw, A. C. (1995) Learning by Association: professional associations as learning agents, *Human Resource Development Quarterly*, **6** (2), 215–26.

Sladek, S. L. (2011) *The End of Membership as We Know It: building the fortune-flipping, must-have association for the next century*, ASAE: The Center for Association Leadership.

Thomas, I., Hegarty, K., Whitman, S. and Macgregor, V. (2012) Professional Associations: their role in promoting sustainable development in Australia, *Journal of Education for Sustainable Development*, **6** (121), 121–36.

Thomas, V. K., Satpathi, C. and Satpathi, J. N. (2010) Emerging Challenges in Academic Librarianship and Role of Library Associations in Professional Updating, *Library Management*, **31** (8–9), 594–609.

Watson, T. (2002) Professions and Professionalism: should we jump off the bandwagon, better to study where it is going?, *International Studies of Management and Organizations*, **32** (2), 93–105.

Wilensky, H. L. (1964) The Professionalization of Everyone?, *American Journal of Sociology*, **70** (September), 137–58.

Wilson, K. M. and Halpin, E. (2006) Convergence and Professional Identity in the Academic Library, *Journal of Librarianship and Information Science*, **38** (June), 79–91.

Woolls, B. (2009) Succession Planning and Passing on Leadership: approaches for library associations. In Varlejs, J. and Walton, G. (eds), *Strategies for Regenerating the Library and Information Profession*, Vol. 139, Walter De Gruyter and Co.

Zaiane, J. R. (2011) Global Information Ethics in LIS: an examination of select national library association English-language codes of ethics, *Journal of Information Ethics*, **20** (2), 25–41.

Zverevich, V. V. (1992) Contribution of Library Associations to the Preparation of Legislation: problems and perspectives, *Nauchnye-Tekhnicheskie Biblioteki*, **1**, 24–7.

CHAPTER 8

And the walls came tumbling down … The library profession confronts all-invasive new managerialism

Colin Storey

Introduction

In response to the editor's request to offer personal reflections on the changes in library management since the 1970s, it is important to begin by stating the author's background, and thus, what this chapter offers. The author began his career as a library assistant in a large, UK public library system in 1970. After graduating from library school he worked in a small, 13-staff college library in the 1970s with two other professionals and then moved on successively to two larger academic libraries in the UK over a period of 16 years. In 1988 the author moved to Hong Kong, and in 2000 became the University Librarian of the Chinese University of Hong Kong (CUHK), a multi-site academic library with 200 staff, four million print volumes and four million e-books. The author retired in December 2012. While Hong Kong academic libraries might at first seem exotic and unrepresentative exemplars for a discussion on library management, it should be noted that the majority of the eight publicly funded tertiary institutions in the very international Hong Kong China Special Administrative Region (SAR) are consistently listed in the *Times Higher Education Supplement* of the world's top 200 universities – indeed three of them are regularly in the top 40. Hitherto, the Hong Kong library environment has been a cosmopolitan melting-pot for library professionals with master's degrees and subsequent experience predominantly acquired in North America, Australasia and the UK. Generally, the abiding priorities in Hong Kong universities reflect a state-of-the-art common world-view in management, teaching, research and the now much-vaunted 'student experience'.

This chapter is not a comprehensive discourse on management sciences or a complete recent history of management theory in libraries. Rather, it is an unapologetically personal take on the changes in management in academic libraries in public sector tertiary institutions as observed over a 40-year career. If the opinions expressed here are considered solipsistic and reductionist, so be it. At the very least, they are honest reflections born of experience. The chapter ends with some suggestions on managing continual change that would be applicable in any library sector.

Years of fundamental change

There were fundamental changes in academic library management from what may be broadly termed 'traditional to modern' at the end of the 20th century and into the 21st. It is posited here that during this period four major developments occurred to alter fundamentally the environments within which librarians worked.

First, the arrival of the new e- and digital technologies – particularly the web, full-text, imaging and single-string search capabilities – set librarians on the back foot in terms of securing their own destinies as valid and contributing professionals within their reader communities.

Second, and in parallel, there was a massive expansion in the numbers of universities and student worldwide in the 1970s and 1980s. Elite institutions became mass institutions. This trend was followed by a long and debilitating decline in funding and income in the 1990s and 2000s, owing to wildly fluctuating economic conditions. In many parts of the world these repeated downward funding trends came to be rather wearily known as 'the cuts'.

Third, a whole slew of new legislation in developed societies revolutionized the workplace: equality of opportunity, anti-discrimination measures, copyright, freedom of information and so on.

Fourth, successive waves of theory infused – some would say infected – the organizational structures of public sector institutions. These theories emanated from the burgeoning number and ubiquity of new schools of business, of management, of social sciences and so on. The new ideas were first tried and tested by the graduates of these schools, out to make a name for themselves in the commercial sector.

The result of these four developments? Universities, predominantly in the public sector, willingly or unwillingly transformed themselves into corporate and competitive business ventures wherein the financial balance sheet of economic return was unprecedentedly and strictly set against that of intellectual endeavour. University managers imported business practices and e-based structures from their business-school-educated counterparts and ICT professionals in the private sector to underwrite donor-funding initiatives, lucrative research bids and league-table success. It became the norm for many university senior vice-presidents and pro-vice-chancellors to be promoted from the business and social science schools as permanent managers to assist in handling variable and sometimes wholly unpredictable external funding, making a mockery of individual institutional imperatives and long-term planning initiatives. A 'new managerialism' in universities became all pervasive. While still routinely praising their libraries as the beating hearts of their universities, senior academics had long identified them as expensive cost centres – 'A bottomless money pit!' exclaimed one president. Their libraries were peopled by professionals on academic or academic-related salaries and conditions of service whose daily work and expertise were not fully or sometimes even remotely understood. In the new environment, academic libraries and their staff became a prime focus of attention for detailed external appraisal and consultancy.

Many changes ensued in the way academic libraries were managed, leading to a brave, modern world for librarians. The library walls came tumbling down, leaving the librarians themselves, their activities and their services wide open to continuous scrutiny and redirection. Librarians were required to be willing activists in or unwilling witnesses to the transformation of their organizations – but in a way that did not render them totally unrecognizable from their former identities. Emerging from a rather comfortable and cloistered existence, librarians confronted this invasiveness in a realistic and positive manner – and in a predominantly evolutionary rather than revolutionary way.

The sure world of 'traditional' library management

I hate work. Libraries are a quite pleasant way of earning a living. Dismal prospects though! ... Another thing that might be said is that librarianship,

with its blend of administration and academic interest, is one of the most
varied of the egg-head professions.

(Philip Larkin [1922–85], British poet and university librarian,
who regularly slept through his institution's senate meetings.
Quoted by John Shakespeare,
Times Literary Supplement, 3 April 2009, 12f)

In the early 1970s, the only new technology demonstrated for a period of
a single hour in a whole semester in one UK library school was the
newfangled medium of the punched card. Students would hold pencils
through a bunch of cards, then release the cards and watch the pencils
'automatically' sort the cards. This was highlighted as a future trend, but
since personal computers and even minicomputers (small mainframes)
were not available, any kind of computer technology was simply out of
reach for anyone other than those working in large research computer
centres.

As far as management theory was concerned, courses concentrated on
the practicalities of library administration and throughput – acquisition,
cataloguing, reference management and so on – rather than on the
strategic management of facilities and finances, or even the day-to-day
management of personnel. In this regard, the only thing the author
remembers being told in a library management course was that 'library
assistants were human with human feelings and should be treated as
such'. These were wise words, but hardly a comprehensive grounding for
what lay ahead for a new professional manager.

Professional librarians arrived in their first assignments and learnt
management informally, by watching; either emulating or distancing
themselves from the actions and motivations of more experienced
colleagues. Unlike today, at the outset there were very few external staff-
development opportunities for learning strategic management. This
wholly paper-based working environment had been evolving slowly and
very surely for over 100, maybe 5000, years. The majority of librarians
had always worked hard; in very busy circulation departments the
atmosphere had never been relaxed. However, librarians were trusted
professionals who were left very much to their own devices by the
institutions in which they worked. A few scenes and vignettes from the
1970s personally witnessed by the author give a flavour of this
environment:

- A locally celebrated head of a public branch library spent his entire existence in his back office writing poetry.
- A nearly retired head of cataloguing arrived at 8.55am on the dot every weekday, changed into carpet slippers, catalogued an average of 30 books, and at 4.55pm on the dot changed back into his street shoes and walked out, perhaps without having spoken a dozen words to anyone.
- A new professional librarian was watched in an amused fashion by very experienced circulation desk paraprofessionals (a term not used then) as she ran after the university's deputy president in an effort to retrieve an on-call book (the deputy president was so keen to keep the book for one more night, he vaulted over the 3M library security gates in the getaway chase).
- A city chief librarian was approached by a reader in his central public library who asked for directions to the reference room. He abruptly pointed to a teenager nearby and retorted, 'Ask him – he's a library assistant!' (So much for reader service. But at least he recognized one of his own library assistants.)
- Such were the vagaries of public funding that when an external validating body insisted that an institution should spend more on its library collections, a vast sum of money was made available to be spent and cleared just three weeks before the end of the financial year. To avoid losing the new money, aside from adopting the fairly standard practice of forward-buying journal subscriptions, the only solution was to buy the complete print set of the *National Union Catalog*. It is doubtful that more than a handful of people used it in the 20 years before the web made it largely redundant.

Then, as now, the institution's academic managers administered an organization made up of several disparate groups of professionals. Along with the academics and their students, there were librarians, facility managers, accountants, student support people, registrars and personnel officers (thankfully, not then called by the dehumanizing term 'human resources'). Driven by the huge expansion in higher education and cushioned by concomitant increased budgets and new buildings, these mutually respectful groups were allowed the freedom to get on with their jobs without much hindrance. The academic staff were also trusted, and left to teach and research; if it took a lifetime to publish just one single *magnum opus*, or indeed never to complete it, so be it. There was an abiding spirit of collegiality.

Change was of course not entirely absent from the academy before the 1980s. Library practices have never been subject to total ossification. Obvious developments in libraries included 'next big things' such as the audiovisual (AV) material fad, which was driven by the establishment of educational technology departments in universities (their expensive TV and AV set-ups mostly failed to make the promised revolutionary impact). Yet, at the ground level in universities, new technology only really took hold in the 1980s in the shape of affordable minicomputers to drive the early forerunners of integrated library systems, followed by the first Apple Macs and personal computers (PCs) suddenly plonked on individual staff desks. Again, ICT initiatives were resourced by ever-expanding higher education funding and readily accepted by library managers who immediately saw the immense benefits of online systems to their end-user communities. Library front-line staff members were sometimes intimidated by their first experience of the new technology, which was often poorly introduced and plagued by slow response times and bugs. As one experienced library assistant said in 1980, 'I do not want that screen between me and the reader!'

Doing more for less: the 'new managerialism' and the library profession

> Cock-sure certainty is the source of much that is worst in our present world, and it is something of which the contemplation of history ought to cure us, not only or chiefly because there were wise men in the past, but because so much that was thought wisdom turned out to be folly – which suggests that much of our own supposed wisdom is no better.
>
> I do not mean to maintain that we should lapse into lazy scepticism. We should hold our beliefs and hold them strongly.
>
> (Russell, 1961, 536)

As regards the four post-1970s developments noted above – the arrival of new technologies, the expansion of universities and funding fluctuations, new legislation and the invasion of new managerialism – the first three are well recognized. While all factors are interrelated, the main focus here is on the fourth development, managerialism.

The *Oxford English Dictionary* defines 'managerialism' as 'Belief in or reliance on the use of professional managers in administering or planning an activity', and quotes a further refinement: 'the belief that commercial management principles have the answers to all organizational problems'. In a report released in the UK that looked at this effect upon universities, the research leader, Rosemary Deem, noted that 'Professionals are subjected to a rigorous regime of external accountability in which continuous monitoring and audit of performance and quality are dominant' (Deem, 2005, 6f). There were obvious and immediate doubts about any 'viable trade-off between managerial control and professional autonomy':

> 'New managerialism' usually refers to practices commonplace in the private sector, particularly the imposition of a powerful management body that overrides professional skills and knowledge. It keeps discipline under tight control and is driven by efficiency, external accountability and monitoring, and an emphasis on standards.
>
> (*THES*, 2001)

By the 1990s, the response by university managers to the growth of a competitive mass market for self-funding students and a worldwide search for research income was to look to the private sector for techniques for tight internal and external organizational and fiscal control. This trend was accelerated by sudden reductions in long-standing government funding streams. It was hoped that such measures would transform the universities' hitherto highly bureaucratic, introspective bodies into dynamic and accountable corporate enterprises; learning organizations that would climb up the newly introduced university league tables. As one fierce UK critic of this whole process noted:

> In reality, the overriding aim is to bring the universities to heel: to change their character, to make them conform to market ideology. Universities must be made into businesses, selling a product to customers: if they reduce costs and increase sales, they make a profit; if they don't, they go bust. Profit is the only indefeasible goal, competition the only effective mechanism.
>
> (Collini, 2013)

Staff members, be they high-flying academics or middle-management librarians, were no longer left alone or trusted to get on with their jobs. Systems for constant target monitoring, internal marketing, sanctioning and rewarding, reporting and appraisal of departments and individuals were beefed up or introduced. Rather than 'manage' their colleagues' work, many academics had traditionally preferred to negotiate around each other in sophisticated collegiate networks. Each department minded its own business in its own academic silo. Given the very nature of their jobs, librarians, for their part, had the advantage of already being experienced in managing staff and resources and being oriented to service the whole academic community. They responded quite quickly to the new regimes. There was little choice in the matter anyway. The overall ideological environment of the universities changed, though for the most part internal structures did not radically alter (Brown with Carasso, 2013; McGettigan, 2013). Once they had become familiar, the new procedures soon settled down as the norm.

Through a series of waves of mounting external pressure, the progress towards a pervasive managerialist environment was a slow but steady one, leading to the current style of capable and willing openness, but, alas, with more administrative paperwork and less time for reflection. Regarding the growth of managerialism, five examples of initiatives imported by or imposed upon librarians will suffice.

Total quality management

Librarians began to look at the quality of their service in terms of regarding the reader, or user, as 'the customer'. An improvement in quality services would come as a direct result of continuous analysis of customers' needs by all levels of staff. This idea has actually had some traction and has proved to have a long legacy. The use of the word 'customer' rather than 'reader' is now, unfortunately, commonplace in academic libraries, though in the UK and the USA this is perhaps understandable, as students take out heavy personal loans to fund their studies. More positively, the expressions 'quality service' and 'fitness for purpose' are now firmly entrenched in the academy.

Business process re-engineering

Re-engineering first necessitated a systematic review and fundamental rethinking of every department's and individual's work mission, with a view to cutting all unnecessary, unproductive work habits and practices. The re-engineering team was often led by an external person. If this was the case, the examination nearly always began with the library's technical services division, since this was a process-led production line that any non-librarian could recognize. The less mechanistic and more intuitive work in front-line services such as reference proved much more challenging and mysterious for non-librarians and was often poorly researched by outsiders. The overall aim was to streamline efficiency towards the common goal of a quality service. The goals were a willingness to accept and embrace change and to build organizational structures to allow continuous change.

Outsourcing and the internal market

While re-engineering toughened all librarians for future, deeper, external scrutiny, it was technical services colleagues who mostly felt the brunt of early re-engineering projects. Many of their activities were outsourced, such as the use in acquisitions and binding of book approval plans and purchase of shelf-ready materials. Long, sunny afternoons on the reference desk, selecting books by ploughing through printed book lists and review journals, mostly became a distant memory.

The growth of the internal market often came in tandem with the re-engineering/outsourcing initiative. Department heads were given a greater degree of independence to administer their now devolved one-line budgets, but were required to buy and sell services from and to other departments within their own institution. This became particularly important in facilities and buildings management.

Mission, vision and the service pledge

In many libraries, the re-engineering process heralded the arrival of the all-pervasive mission statement and its shorter sibling, the vision statement. The composition or review of an organization's mission was founded upon the individual mission statement of each and every employee. On being asked to write a mission statement, one young first professional simply wrote, 'My mission is to do my job well!' Alas, many statements were much longer. The vision statement was in turn a more snappy summation of the mission statement – a bite-sized piece for library users to ingest even if they never read anything else produced by the library. The service pledge was often written and promoted as a result of mission and vision projects. Systematically, and for the first time for many academic librarians, finalizing the pledge involved direct and sustained consultation with various types and levels of library reader individually or in focus groups.

On the negative side, it was now commonplace for new, sometimes nearly meaningless, jargon to infect the academy. By the end of a career, any experienced library manager could write a statement almost blind-folded, using all the right current buzzwords and phrases: metrics (never now 'statistics'); footfalls (never now 'gate-counts'); empowerment (ugh!); quality-assured outcomes; the student journey etc., etc. ... There was also a tendency to use strings of nouns as adjectives, and to redundancy and repetition – habits borrowed from commercial marketing. To compose one absurd example (there is meaning in here somewhere if any first-year undergraduate, or even a campaigner for simple English, could find it),

Peopled by experience-led, standard-bearer information professionals, your one-stop shop learning hub will provide a pedagogy-rich, heuristically-sound user interface through the dynamic and flexible medium of a multi-faceted, value-added, individually-tailored virtual and real environment with the aim of empowering multi-level customers in the timely pursuit of their stated life goals and accompanying them through the stress points of their academic journeys to the off-ramp of their success.

On the positive side, these were indeed the first real steps towards a fuller realization by the library profession as a whole about the selective but crucial integration of marketing tools into the service culture in order to promote understanding of what librarians could do for people, and to encourage and to broadcast effective and popular use of their services among students, teachers and researchers. The embracing of marketing by librarians has led logically to their current avid use of social and mobile media, although at the outset many students wondered out loud what the heck the library was doing registering on *their* informal social networks.

Management consultancies

A major consequence of all this activity was the rise of the management consultancy in university service departments. Senior academic managers perceived that they could get a professional and unbiased view of what was actually happening and how money was being spent on the ground floor of their institutions. There are some fundamental questions about the new managerialism involving consultancies that need to be addressed.

In the outsourcing documentation for a consultant it is of course a prerequisite that the consultant be ably qualified. *Recruitment* consultants prove to be least qualified in the library arena. They are hardly ever library trained and, once hired, their first act is to ring up librarians and ask them if they are interested in the advertised job. If they are not, then the next questions are, 'Do you know anyone else who might be interested? Do you have any comment on our advert and on the content of the job?' The library staff can end up acting as unpaid consultants to their very own organization's over-paid management consultants.

If they are not professional librarians themselves, do consultants simply sell back the information supplied to them as suggestions for service improvements and cost-effectiveness? Even if they are professional librarians, does anyone ever balance the cost of hiring them against the cost of staff preparing documents and holding meetings to educate them on the unique features of the institution? Every hour with a management consultant is one hour less serving readers.

'Painting-by-numbers', so 'management-by-numbers'. A consultancy can be a process of *reductio ad absurdum*, all bean counting and no humanity. Where are the soft words like passion, diplomacy, love of the work and understanding?

What of the dangers in undermining staff morale? By sending in a management consultant, senior managers may be thought to be also sending the message, 'Yes, I know you have repeatedly told us what you do and how you do it. But, well, we simply don't believe you, we don't trust you. You're too expensive, so we're sending in an outsider whom we trust more than we trust our own staff.' The negative effects can be declining corporate trust and discretion.

One more observation: if the consultant were to file a report that the library management had submitted requests for additional manpower and financial resources that were considered to be unrealistic and over-blown, then surely the logical action for the commissioning senior academic managers would be to ask for the department head's immediate resignation on the grounds of new-managerial incompetence?

The usual result of a consultancy is a downsizing and/or rationalization of staffing and resources – surely an aim of any consultancy in the first place – thus rendering the whole process of 'open and objective investigation' morally suspect. On balance, and unlike many other initiatives, the overall impacts of external consultancies are not thought here to have had positive effects.

There are more new managerial models that could be discussed, such as strategic planning, ISO 9000 and the author's particular *bête noir*: knowledge management (an unnecessarily imported concept rendered meaningless when applied by university librarians to serve the unbound intellects of their academic colleagues). Of course, advice on new ways to manage flows out of a never-ending stream of publication, brings with it opportunities and/or threats. Hayes (2001) gives a good review of the various models available for planning and decision making. From early on, some new practices were adopted unbidden, independently introduced by librarians into their own organizations. This was done explicitly in order to improve services; implicitly to forestall any idea that librarians were untrained and disengaged professional managers. Conversely, when senior academic managers insisted upon imposing their new-managerialist strategies on the library, this usually meant one thing: they questioned what they considered to be the loose statistics and anecdotal satisfaction surveys that librarians traditionally forwarded to prove the worth of their services. Fluctuating funding meant that senior managers were continually challenged to balance budgets, and so they correspondingly challenged their junior colleagues in all departments. One senior academic said to the author:

> *Every* programme or project brought to me is purported to be for the benefit of the university. But all proposals bear a financial cost. Everyone wants more money. So no one should bring a proposal to me without a cost-benefit analysis; this is now the abiding factor. Do more for less and give me the bottom line! For example, the level of budget earmarked for staff development in the library is larger than many small academic departments which undertake the main business of this university: teaching and research. Why send a librarian rather than an academic to a conference abroad?

The new processes always involved time-consuming interviews and report writing. The 'executive summary' on two bite-sized pages of A4 was born to provide busy senior university managers with the gist of what their state-of-the-art librarians had achieved. Most new trends had a life-span of about three to five years before something newer came along to supersede them (Ponzi and Keonig, 2002). These latest ideas were often regarded by academic library staff as short-term fads. Managers imposed *upon* staff rather than engaged *with* them in any real practical sense. For the staff members involved in any given initiative, there were obvious gains in having to stand back and reflect objectively on daily work and service priorities. After the final report was written and some job titles were changed in an organizational reshuffle, life soon settled down. Nevertheless, the days of predictable and safe 'traditional' academic library management were well and truly over. For the most part, academic librarians have reacted calmly and diligently to the ever-changing environment. Their professional composure remained intact in the face of welcome and unwelcome attention, even as their worth within the academy – once taken as read – was now expected to be routinely questioned.

Common-sense library management skills

> However, not everything that can be counted counts, and not everything that counts can be counted.
>
> (Often attributed to Einstein, and possibly to Cameron, 1963, 13)

The author has had little recourse to management textbooks over the years. 'More's the pity!' some colleagues might observe. Some aphorisms from the management gurus have indeed rung true; for example, 'Formula for success: under promise and over deliver' (Tom Peters). However, reductive reasoning like this, based on business school professors' bulleted PowerPoint presentations, has been studiously avoided in favour of spending a career watching and learning from the best (and the worst) library managers in their efforts to make sense of the people and situations that confront them.

Notwithstanding his opinions about reductive thinking and bean counting in business and life-affirmation books, the author will break his own rules and offer advice that seems to him to make some kind of sense, but is routinely ignored or wholly unknown by so many people striving to use what intelligence they have to the full. It is by no means a unique standpoint that the path to successful management advanced here is heavily biased towards behavioural and personal interaction with fellow human beings, rather than towards mechanistic and spreadsheet-based decision making. This advice might contain some obvious truisms. It might be instinctively felt to be old fashioned, but only because the professional body of librarians has collectively adhered to many of these tenets for more than a hundred years (it is suggested here that the collective noun for librarians should of course be 'a volume'). These management traditions spring from deep and hard-won experience on how a volume of librarians should conduct and offer services to their communities; many remain wholly valid and should not be jettisoned. They can remain a bulwark against new-managerialist pressures.

If this advice rings true, supervising librarians will feel more self-assured in building up experience and skills that will stand them in good stead in times of disruptive change. It is hoped that these ten broad principles will prompt them to instil common-sense attitudes in their younger and less-experienced colleagues. Those who will become the successors in the management of a given library should be encouraged not just by pursuing formal staff development paths but, crucially, by watching and learning from their effective line managers. Naturally, questions about the actions and attitudes of colleagues should be reflected upon by *all* managers on a daily basis: 'How did she handle that complaint from a reader?' 'Did he choose the right method of improving the performance of that difficult member of staff?' 'Could the chair of that meeting have organized it better so that it could have ended an hour earlier and still be productive?' and so on.

Humility

Exercise humility and remember six basic tenets: (1) no one person is indispensable in any workplace; (2) unless you are very luckily placed, do not expect to finish everything in a long career or leave any legacy; (3) the best people are those who treat everyone with respect – the worst people are the pretentious, many of whom peak too soon in their lives, and subsequently live a long and disappointed career afterlife; (4) do not be too pushy with your boss with too many ideas too soon; (5) never stop promoting and explaining what professional librarians can do for their communities in adding value to their reading and searching; and (6) do not be afraid to listen, be open, rethink, copy the best and be flexible – and still be your own person.

Perseverance

Do not let them see you coming; keep them guessing throughout your career. Some of the very best managers turn out to be those who were considered surprise promotions and then, when necessary, artfully resist the boss's pressure to change against their better professional judgement.

Do not let ambition eat you up. Take your time, and success will come. Never stand on anyone's head to get to the next rung of the ladder. Conversely, you may think you can do your disorganized boss's job better, but be careful of what you wish for. There may be aspects of work further up the organization that you will hate. A promotion to an executive position will mean more administration and politics, and less in-library work.

Instinct

A manager needs political nous or a 'nose' to distinguish what issues need immediate attention and what can be left to lie fallow. This is inborn or comes with experience. Some unfortunate people do not have it and will never acquire it – it makes them very ineffective managers.

Momentum

Maintaining momentum is crucial yet very difficult. How many new strategic or tactical work changes can any library staff take in a week? Yet, if there are no initiatives, momentum will be lost and stagnation will set in. Keep pushing and moving forward, but note that there is no shame in staying slightly behind the curve and avoiding flashy fads.

Let others claim the state-of-the-art and the leading edge. By all means use the persuasive marketing tools at your disposal, but do not shout from the rooftops about an ongoing project before a successful outcome is assured. Do not experiment on readers with untried ideas in order to advance a career. Similarly, do not be an absentee landlord by constantly

cruising the conference circuit; be there, in the library, most of the time –
not somewhere else. The unique community of readers being served is of
paramount concern. Concentrate on guiding the internal teams at various
levels to succeed in that service, and ignore how it looks to other librarians
in other libraries.

Patient reflection

In the vast majority of cases no challenge in librarianship is important
enough that it cannot wait one day. Talk it over with sensible, objective
colleagues, or, when a problem seems intractable, sleep on it. If no solution
miraculously presents itself by the next morning (and it will often do so),
always consider the Daoist way forward as a serious option – *wuwei* 无为
– do nothing! Some problems melt away with time (though some can come
back and bite).

If a deadline cannot be met, or the assigned task seems too hard, any
boss will be reasonable if appealed to for help. Conversely, when asked
when a task can be completed, always allow a little more deadline time.
Do not say '5pm today' if the boss will be satisfied with '5pm tomorrow'.
It is always useful to wait until the last day and submit actually on
deadline. A thought might occur or an event might happen on deadline
day, resulting in required amendments. When a solution cannot be
found and the boss's help is needed, offer at least one suggestion to
him/her as an option.

Never go empty handed and just dump the problem on the boss's desk.
Similarly, never forward a memo or an e-mail to a boss without
demonstrating that some thought has been put into the matter first and
a recommendation has been made for possible action. In universities, since
senior managers are normally first and foremost academics, they are
happiest critiquing written work. Write briefing reports in the style they
are used to when reading academic submissions. Adopt an approach to
line-management meetings with them that is more akin to advanced
postgraduate supervisions.

Never impulsively send an angry e-mail or memo, or make an
impassioned phone call to anyone, before careful reflection. This does not
mean to say that anger or frustration should not occasionally be expressed.
Anger, real or feigned (better to fake it), can be a very useful tool to achieve
results, though disappointment or standing one's professional ground as

weapons in the amphitheatre of management can be more powerful and less destructive.

Respect

Regard the people whom *you report to* as at least as intelligent as you are, even if they are not. Serve without being servile. Regard the people who *report to you* as at least as intelligent as you are, even if they are not. Try to treat all people fairly, working *with them* not *for you*; most people will respond positively. *Always* say hello to staff members on first encounter on any day. Those who try to undermine or take advantage of trust, flexibility and openness in their line managers are only fooling themselves. There is no need to bother to tell them that the games they play are self-evident – just let them carry on digging a hole for themselves. As in life, so in management – right will eventually prevail. As Martin Luther King Jr said, 'because you shall reap what you sow ... because the arc of the moral universe is long but it bends towards justice'.

If negative people repeatedly do not follow sane direction, then it is they who are at fault. They need to make their own mind up about their future. Sometimes a member of staff's only option is the realization that he/she just has to leave and find a better job or a better boss elsewhere.

Since no one person is indispensable, try very hard never to deny anyone a day's leave if they want it, even (and especially) if you are given only an hour's notice. If a member of staff has a problem with their family, tell them that family is the most important thing in the world and give them leeway to sort out the immediate problem *before* any work priorities.

Discipline

What to a manager is a very obvious statement or request may not be so obvious to those who receive it. Detailed and repeated explanation and persuasion may be necessary for reluctant staff members, even when it is not directly for the benefit of the service but entirely for theirs. Unless it is part of a formal legal procedure, never reprimand anyone in front of other people. Even in private, you will find that expressing simple disappointment at an individual's performance may be much more effective than any severe reprimand.

Delegation

Delegate jobs – but *not* responsibility for them if people mess up. When people make a mistake, find a solution – not someone to blame. Autopsies on failures are totally counter-productive. In truth, linking delegation and responsibility is an oxymoron: is *everything* bad that happens in a department the manager's fault, and everything good absolutely nothing to do with him or her?

Nurture

Recruit new staff without favour to fit in with a team. Assuming that they possess the right qualifications (otherwise why shortlist?), the key attributes are openness and a sense of humour – they will need them for the challenges in training and service to come.

No matter where they are reassigned and however much they are retrained, the hardest people to motivate are the ones rated average to good, always doing a reasonable job so they cannot be sanctioned but, alas, having nothing in them or no motivation to allow them to do a first-rate job and progress up the ladder. The manager has to live with this frustration, but, alas, so do they. Give the keen ones, who want to develop themselves for their own benefit and for the service, all the mentoring and assistance possible. There might be accusations of favouritism. Be aware of this, though it would be inhuman not to like some people better than others, or to prefer working with those who respond positively rather than with an organization's lost souls.

Integrity

And finally, remember that professionals do not actively set any fixed limits to daily work or regard a job description as written in concrete. However, draw a moral and professional line in work and do not go beyond it. For a boss, this line can be further back than many people's. Managers call it pragmatism, a willingness to listen and flexibility. Others might call it inconsistency, insincerity, hypocrisy – even mendacity. As Runciman expounded in his book on political hypocrisy, it is important to cultivate a seamless habit of virtue, even if you have to fake it (2008). Whatever the definition, the line has to be consistently drawn in order for you to have any authority, although total, unalloyed consistency is symptomatic of a prosaic and prejudiced mind.

Confronting new managerialism with tradition and passion

A man may surely be allowed to take a glass of wine by his own fireside.
(Richard Brinsley Sheridan, on being encountered calmly drinking a
glass of wine in the street, while watching his theatre,
the Drury Lane, burn down on 24 February 1809)

Broadly adhering to these principles when living through the pressures
from senior managers to adopt new practices that may prove long or short
lived can lead to a measure of success in sustaining the real foundations
for an adaptable and responsive service in any library sector. The evidence
for this lies in the author's own experience. In the privileged position of
being the director of CUHK Library over 12 busy years, the author saw
positive and negative changes imposed upon the library from external
pressure. There were also many positive changes initiated and wrought
by the librarians themselves, who subtly or unsubtly stuck to their guns
with a passionate eye for the traditions of the profession.

By the 2000s at CUHK, the senior management team was made up of
four people: the director; the deputy, who looked after ICT and the
branches; the head of public services; and the head of technical services.
As would be expected in any workplace, all four had very different
personalities. The two clear common factors that united them were, first,
a deep commitment to the profession and its future and, second, an even
more fundamental loyalty to the institution they worked for. By 2010, the
total time served at CUHK by the four individuals was over 80 years.
Service commitment on this level can be taught, but it can take time and
some will not respond. The long-term service of these officers did not
nurture stagnant thinking – quite the reverse. Yet collectively the team
was gravely suspicious of anything that smacked of faddish proposals that
would not dovetail with the innate culture of the university and thus with
its community of readers. In short, this dream team had *passion*. This
caring concern permeated the layers of line managers, supervisors and
younger, less-experienced but enthusiastic staff members throughout the
flattened team hierarchy. Of course, some staff did not buy into the
planned strategy and its very soft approach; nothing is perfect when
keeping to the main road, avoiding diversions and only rerouting when

team discussions on evolving circumstances deem it clearly necessary.

These common factors created a united front for always wanting to move the service forward and for responding to the calls by the senior academic managers for more openness and more systematic and universally recognizable reporting methods. From the readers' side, CUHK Library was thought of in a kindly way. Many of the professors were alumni of the institution and had fond memories of the library as it was (read, 'always had been'). While this could cause problems – particularly when planning to change internal library environments – generally speaking, this again gave a very soft, humanistic advantage to the library staff in explaining what it was trying to do. Despite some few loud voices to the contrary, the professors and students were generally happy to see the library walls tumbling down for a more open environment as long as they were informed and consulted. In short, they cared too.

The major initiative in the 2000s was the building of an extension to the main library and creating modern, 24-hour, dynamic learning spaces (discussed by the author in detail in a forthcoming 2015 paper for *Library Management*). The building opened with revamped services in late 2012, and subsequently received an architectural award. More importantly, by any measure (and especially by the University's own graduate exit surveys), satisfaction with the library continues to grow significantly – evidence of the passionate commitment shown by succeeding generations of CUHK Library staff.

Naturally, such a massive project was not without major challenges. The planning was primarily overseen by senior academic managers who had little experience of librarians joining in intense debates on what was necessary for teaching and research. The initial logical reaction of some university leaders was simplicity itself: sharpen up the whole operation; get rid of all the print; therefore cheaper storage costs; therefore fewer library staff needed; therefore a whole lot cheaper all round. Constant outside interference and scattergun negative comments can engender a jaded cynicism in library managers ('None of what you propose will work and it is too expensive!' 'I'm a scientist, I need my print-runs – will they be in some inaccessible locked store?' 'A food and drink café – in the library?'). Yet management is about outflanking the imposition of limits. It is about standing back (or losing sleep) and objectively analysing what is actually happening at a given juncture when negativity and doubt arise. It is about patiently choosing a future time and method to convert or subvert the nay-sayers.

Tradition and passion in library management are not to be considered old fashioned or weak. Tradition is not to be confused with the cynicism of a tired, old, slipper-shod fuddy-duddy muttering in the corner. In terms of the valuable and hard-won traditional tenets of librarianship, any library manager should instinctively understand that innovations need long-term traction if they are to have any meaning or use for readers. A passion to serve also transcends the transitory; it eschews jargon-ridden, bullet-point thinking and the shallow, latest vibe. Tradition and passion, then, are formidable weapons in the library manager's arsenal. They are attributes that are recognized and respected by any person of even modest intellect. Tradition and passion allow librarians to stand ready to deal effectively and patiently with anything the new managerialists may propose, dispose or impose.

References

Brown, R. with Carasso, H. (2013) *Everything for Sale? The marketisation of UK higher education*, Routledge.

Cameron, W. B. (1963) *Informal Sociology: a casual introduction to sociological thinking*, Random House.

Collini, S. (2013) Sold Out, *London Review of Books*, **20** (20 October), 3–12, www.lrb.co.uk/v35/n20/stefan-collini/sold-out.

Deem, R. (2005) *'New Managerialism' and the Management of UK Universities*, Lancaster University: Economic and Social Research Council, www.esrc.ac.uk/my-esrc/grants/R000237661/read.

Hayes, R. M. (2001) *Models for Library Management Decision-making and Planning*, Academic Press.

McGettigan, A. (2013) *The Great University Gamble: money, markets and the future of higher education*, Pluto Press.

Ponzi, L. J. and Koenig, M. (2002) Knowledge Management: another management fad?, *Information Research*, **8**, (1), paper no. 145.

Runciman, D. (2008) *Political Hypocrisy: the mask of power from Hobbes to Orwell and beyond*, Princeton University Press.

Russell, B. (1961) *The Basic Writings of Bertrand Russell*, Routledge.

THES (2001) Outbreak of 'New Managerialism' Infects Faculties, *Times Higher Education Supplement*, 20 July, https://www.timeshighereducation. co.uk/news/outbreak-of-new-managerialism-infects-faculties/164003.article/.

CHAPTER 9

What is behind the meaning of disruption? Or, thinking of management strategies from the outside

Steve O'Connor

It is important to write about the management of libraries. The literature is extensive and often reflective of the era when it was written, radiating much wisdom, individual perspective, theory, research and experience. It is also grounded in and informed by many social, informational and technological currents. Embedded within it are the best management theories, strategies and pathways, with the aim to achieve excellence in current and future planning and in the application of change. Indeed, change management has almost become a discipline in its own right and will most likely remain so for the foreseeable future, as successful change requires the most careful planning and management. The aim of this chapter is to reflect on changes that have happened in and to libraries, to understand the extent to which they have been 'disruptive' and to advocate for the literature on change to be more forward looking and less prescriptive.

The chapters in this volume were commissioned to explore most aspects of what is meant by 'library management', but in disruptive times. The term 'disruptive' is used in the context in which Clayton Christenson popularized it: 'describes a process by which a product or service takes root initially in simple applications at the bottom of a market and then relentlessly moves up-market, eventually displacing established competitors'.[1] This will be explored in more detail later in this chapter.

The central thesis of this chapter is that libraries are very vulnerable to fundamental 'disruptive change', but that such change is currently not being recognized as anything other than simple change. If this thesis is sound, then library managers need to look to planning for the future of libraries in a significantly different way. Many libraries are working hard on change, but their plans are often limited to the next annual budget cycle. They need to look beyond the limits of this annual cycle and plan for a radically different future. It is the present author's contention that this future can be achieved within a planning cycle of no more than three to five years. Most library planning does not allow for a future that is even marginally, let alone radically, different from what exists now. This in itself is a problem and an area of great vulnerability for libraries. Justifying the continued existence of the library without having any story about the future leaves the field completely open to other stories from areas outside the library's control. It is as if the library has no clear vision of the future, of possible futures or of what its particular community of users really needs.

On the outside, looking in

If they understand this 'disruptive' context, library managers can think, plan and operate more effectively; they can plan for both the short term and the longer term. In order to achieve this position they need a perspective that both relates to and is beyond the regular management of the library's performance.

Being a librarian necessarily means to be 'on the inside'. We know the 'insider' stories, we understand the language of MARC records, reference interviews, circulation woes and issues such as Open Access (OA). All of these are important to us as insiders. We understand the multitude of acronyms. Our customers, people in support roles in the library (but who are not librarians) and those in allied professions do not think or care about issues or services in the same way that an insider does. These people are 'outsiders'. They see the library world quite differently. In the days when libraries did not face rapid technological and social change the insider reigned supreme, had command of the language and the tools of the library, and spoke with the voice of authority within the library. To assume today that a librarian can speak *ex cathedra* on the topic 'library' and all will be well is an illusion. The traditional library business model is dead, and along with it the idea that this is our territory and ours alone.

An outsider's view is essential when libraries are so engaged with all aspects of 'digital' and 'the library' is no longer necessarily a place. The physical, bricks-and-mortar library is still with us, but the library is also everywhere, through its digital presence. The perspective that an outsider can bring to a problem will often provide that different view that enables a strategic breakthrough.

To illustrate just this point, in 1986 the present author co-wrote an article called 'Attitudes Toward Technology as Predictors of Online Catalog Usage'.[2] The research involved measuring social attitudes toward computers in the context of the introduction of an OPAC into a library. This was research into social psychology in action, and the outsiders' view of professional social psychology profoundly affected the insiders' view on the impact of the OPAC:

> It is clear from the study that although library users, at one level, can give a specific technology a very high level of acceptance, the same users can, at another level, exhibit contrasting attitudes toward computer technology in general. This view of new computer technology has not been subject to intense investigation and yet may have far reaching implications for library managers and practitioners. These attitudes of distrust and positive acceptance can be predictors of acceptance and future usage of OPACs.[3]

The outcomes of the research deepened understanding of the conundrum of library users' accepting a particular library technology while having a profound distrust of the underlying computer technology. This aspect of the introduction of digital technology into libraries had not been considered before. To discover this distrust of a technology on which libraries rely so heavily today was very thought provoking. The users' (i.e. outsiders') views impacted heavily on their understanding of a library application such as the OPAC. In response to this finding, the library subsequently sought to provide its users with as much education as possible about its future plans; to do as much research and planning for the future as possible; to communicate and to market the library to its users as much as it is reasonable to do; and to listen, listen, listen. Listening is the basic skill of marketing, and to adopt the view of the 'outsider looking in' is the best way to achieve significant insights.

Our clients provide us with 'outsider' views of the library, whether at a personal or a professional level – and the two are equally important.

Crowdsourced innovation

InnoCentive[4] is an online service that was established to see how solutions can be found to problems that have eluded highly professional teams of engineers. The problems are detailed on the InnoCentive website and, after some weeks, solutions begin to emerge from both allied and, sometimes, very different professionals. The InnoCentive service states, 'We crowdsource innovation solutions from the world's smartest people, who compete to provide ideas and solutions to important business, social, policy, scientific, and technical challenges.'[5] The outsider's view is still providing innovative and practicable solutions to 'insider' problems!

In both our personal and our professional lives the solutions and directions that we choose have an impact on what we do, on our behaviour and on our perceptions of events and of other people. For the most part, the reasons driving our actions, behaviour or perceptions will be beyond the understanding of the outside world looking in. The outsider's view may hold to a very different set of solutions and directions. If we have knowledge of the diversity of ideas, they can provide a context for development and growth. From individual perspectives come a bewildering array of potential approaches to similar problems. How can we build this diversity of ideas into the library culture? If individuals have unique and sharply different experiences and perspectives, what is to stop them from combining with other, different and acceptable responses to crises? The impetus should be to create new thinking, not to cling to stagnant or derivative thinking. It can be argued that 'same thinking' is not necessarily too limiting so long as there is some genuine viewing of the future from the perspective of an 'outsider', along with the development of different options and not just one perceived future. 'Same thinking' led to the failure of IBM to see the potential of the personal computer (PC) and of Nokia to understand that the smartphone would be far more important than the basic mobile phone. These two global giants both failed to register the potential impact of a small, disruptive technology. Both had the technology within their grasp: MS-DOS in the case of IBM and digital photography in the case of Kodak. The traditional library business model is dead and in this instance the disruptive technology is digital delivery. More on this later.

'Outsider' thinking

Libraries are under threat in a number of ways from a variety of pressures, ranging from financial pressures on their parent institutions to governmental crises affecting library financing and roles, the perceived value of libraries, the impact of the internet, and new publishing practices. The movement of Web 2.0 to Web 3.0, from the current good search capability to the Semantic Web or intelligent searching, provides even more challenges. The role of publishing, the decline of the print newspaper, the conflict between Open Access and subscribed digital content, all require not reactions but thought about where these issues are heading. The rate at which all of these changes have come, and will continue to come, into our field of vision is remarkable. Establishing a range of different futures makes for effective positioning of the library and its services. Therefore library managers need to be adaptable and insightful, and to have leadership qualities and the sheer determination to persevere when they believe that what they are planning is right for their library's situation.

'Outside-in' thinking is a prism through which libraries can begin to see how their clients or customers wish to see the world. It is a tool and a preparation for dealing with disruption. To achieve this kind of future thinking requires a wholly different approach and time horizon from that of the present. It also requires library managers to encourage the user community to lead them to the kind of library that they need.

On a popular level it is said that we are exposed to constant change – and indeed we are. It is the combined rate and extent of massive change that is causing a disorientation in our lives. During the past 100 years preceding generations have also seen fundamental change, but not in such a concentrated way as we are now experiencing it. Clayton Christenson, the promulgator of 'disruptive innovation', describes such innovation or change as 'a process by which a product or service takes root initially in simple applications at the bottom of a market and then relentlessly moves up market, eventually displacing established competitors'.[6] There is little time to reflect and think.

When we take a journey along a familiar route we may experience a complete lack of memory as to how we reached our destination. Nor can we recall the journey itself We will rationalize the journey as just being 'normal', 'same same'. In our professional lives we may look back on how we arrived at the current state of play and believe that the path was straight and almost predictable. We forget that there were many points of decision along the way. There were indeed many points at which we had to decide to go in one direction or another; we had to decide to start a new service in response to a challenge, or to get out of that service; we had to decide, we had to decide. If any of those decisions had been different, it would have led us to a quite different future. Our recall as to how we arrived at the present can be very misleading, but disruption of one sort or another will certainly have occurred.

Christenson has written (and continues to teach) extensively on the subject of change and his seminal work on this topic is probably *The Innovator's Dilemma* (Harper Collins, 1997). The book has become gospel for those seeking to understand how to deal with unprecedented rates of change. Essentially, Christenson alerts us to the need to look for competitors in our businesses and to plan to reorganize or reinvent our business model in response to change.

The traditional library business model, whereby users came to the physical library building for all of their information and study, is stone dead! This is not a difficult argument to make. Publishers and librarians are both in the same business, but with different 'profit' ambitions. But they have shared needs for processes and outcomes. There is more to align with than to disagree about.

Publishers have introduced different business models and processes, but for the most part libraries respond through and are wedded to their existing processes. Both are affected by digital technologies. As library managers, we are easily absorbed by the here and now, the daily grind of this issue or that. But that which we do not see is that to which we should be devoting more attention. This situation demands a different approach to management of our profession, in addition to thinking as an insider. It demands that a significant amount of time should also be spent looking to the three-to-five-year time horizon. What is on that horizon, demanding to be observed and analysed?

The future of publishing

The future of publishing, of writing, for the dissemination of ideas, information and content is the major issue now facing libraries. The issue has many facets and may not be the only or, in the end, the most pressing one. Identification of the real, systemic threats to the 'status quo' that it presents is vital, even if the solutions are not immediately identifiable.

Consider this:

> Characteristics of disruptive businesses, at least in their initial stages, can
> include: lower gross margins, smaller target markets, and simpler products
> and services that may not appear as attractive as existing solutions
> when compared against traditional performance metrics. Because these lower
> tiers of the market offer lower gross margins, they are unattractive to other
> firms moving upward in the market, creating space at the bottom of the
> market for new disruptive competitors to emerge.[7]

Christenson theorizes, on the basis of case studies, that a disruptive
technology will have these characteristics.

In the not-for-profit world in which most libraries function, there is
much evidence of changes impacting on the business model. Some of the
changes emanate from external forces, such as the economy, and even
elections. These economic or political forces are disruptive to the business,
but not disruptive in the sense discussed here. These disruptions to
funding, and even to the purposes of the library, will vary according to the
sector that the library serves. Public libraries in some countries have
suffered swingeing cuts to many aspects of their operations but, generally
speaking, they have been busily responding to the challenges of their
customers and are therefore quite viable in their communities. Special
libraries have suffered variously and thrived. Overall, their success has
been based on the extent to which the librarian or manager has infiltrated
the business needs of the parent organization. Academic libraries continue
to survive, but for the most part do not thrive at all. They survive because
they provide undergraduates with an environment in which to study. In
some countries academic libraries are great status symbols on the
university campus. A larger library reflects the dominant status of the
parent university; the wealth of the institution is reflected in the strength
of the library. Still, academic libraries are vulnerable when the academic
community seriously questions the purpose of the library. Such academics
openly proclaim that they never visit or, indeed, use the library. This
message reaches the senior university administration loudly and clearly.

Consider the following scenarios confronting libraries in the area of
content delivery.

One: if the costs of receiving published content and the variety of modes
of delivery have been steadily increasing, so too have libraries' problems

in fulfilling their work as currently perceived. In other words, libraries are affording less content for their customers. They are being required to be even more discerning as to the choice of content for their customers. If this scenario is carried to a logical conclusion, then publishers will start looking for quite different markets and sources of revenue. Logically, they will also be much more careful about the content that they choose to publish. If libraries acquire less content from publishers, then the availability of research and other content will be severely reduced, despite content continuing to be being published.

Two: if libraries become increasingly captive to publishers and the number of publishers steadily decreases with the narrowing of publisher ownership, this will produce a perfect environment in which disruptive technologies can flourish. Remember that in the 1960s IBM was the player that ignored a small challenger called the PC. In fact, IBM 'gave' (depending on whom you believe) its MS-DOS software to Microsoft. The rest is history. The business giant did not see the humble PC as being any kind of challenger to its power and strength. Christenson's conclusions on disruptive technologies derive from this and other examples. Currently, Open Access via the institutional repository, in evolving policy terms, is changing the embargoed period of new research. This has far-reaching implications for all libraries to re-engage with publishing both as funders and, indeed, as initiators. This is a highly credible scenario that no doubt will be realized in many different iterations and models. In this case Open Access would be the disruptive technology to fundamentally change the nature of publishing and the distribution of information.

Three: if, for 70 years, the traditional publishing business model has created a symbiotic relationship between publishers and libraries, and if the current model is being reinvented, then new and more effective business models could appear that would adversely affect both players. Copyright is under constant reinvention. There are those who say that it will not continue to exist, or will change radically. In the digital world available content is viewed by many as common property for their free use. What would the world of content be like if copyright were no longer as strong and relevant an issue as it is today? The Creative Commons (CC)[8] licence has already started to move the debate along this path.

What if? What if??

In the above three scenarios all players in the publishing industry are potentially vulnerable. Disruption is a very powerful phenomenon. Each of the above scenarios is entirely plausible and their disruptive effects would see very dramatic changes at a library systemic level. They may not happen tomorrow or the next day, but the impact when they do happen will be very dramatic. We need to explore the scenarios that we do not feel comfortable with. We will then gain some real perspective on the matter.

Educating for change

At the level of the individual library it is difficult to plan for the kinds of change envisaged in the scenarios outlined above. The library manager must perform many roles and make many decisions daily in allocating available resources so as to ensure the smooth operation of the library. But a forward picture is needed of what could be, and library departmental managers need to become aware that what has always been so will not remain the same – and soon. Managers who do not even acknowledge that change of such magnitude can and very likely will happen are drowning in inertia.

Educating for change is thus a critical strategy across the profession, both in formal library education and in the workplace. Library educators are facing difficulties within a financially straitened higher education sector, let alone in designing curricula for their programmes. Higher education and formal library education are undergoing fundamental change, and funding is a political issue. There is greater public focus on and support for education up to the age of 18, and less on tertiary education. The result has been significant pressure to shift the burden of costs of higher education onto the user, i.e. the student. We are also seeing a pedagogical change, from face-to-face teaching to the cheaper option of online education. In addition to the advent of MOOCs (massive open online courses), simple online learning programmes such as BlackBoard have become the delivery vehicles for programmes of learning and instruction. These are proprietary systems in which it is difficult to provide library content and to link to wider library resources.

Educating entry-level students for future careers as library managers is not easy. It is pleasing to note the change in emphasis of LIS training programmes so as to achieve a wider focus on information rather than on libraries alone. By this means students are made aware of a wider role for 'libraries' and acquire a better understanding of the pervasive impact of information in the communities served by 'libraries'. The libraries of the future will be very different from those of today.

For library managers who are progressing through their careers, there is a real professional development gap in terms of developing and refining their understanding of the potential future directions of the organizations in which they work. Professional reading and conference attendance will help, of course, but more formal, structured programmes dealing with the future trajectories for libraries are needed. And then there is the issue of the management styles and relationships to people that different generations develop. There is a large literature on the different behaviours of Gen Y as compared, say, with the baby boomers. The two generations will not only see the library differently but will also have different styles of management. The baby boomers are now retiring from their position of dominance, to be replaced by Gen X and the Millennials. This generational change is providing real evidence of differences of approach that could better understand the ways in which libraries should respond to change and shape their service offerings. An excellent paper by Julia Artman, 'Motivating Millennials', discusses what we can learn from generational differences in approaches to and views on management and leadership.[9]

Doing things we do not feel altogether comfortable with

It is ironic that the more pressure libraries come under, the more they seem to have retreated into their own operations, rather than seeking greater engagement with each other in order to reduce costs and improve service offerings. It is almost as if collaboration is acceptable in the good times, but less so in difficult times. Of course, this is a generalization, and it is only slowly becoming the case that back-office operations are being outsourced to library consortia and commercial organizations. The element of collaboration and/or co-operation needs to be so embedded in the organization so that it is perceived as a function of the organization. How can this function improve its service offerings to its clientele? So we could also think about what is acceptable or appropriate for our collective rather than individual library future.

Nimble library organizations need to focus totally on their customers or clients. If this necessitates restructuring the library, that is what is should be done. Outside-in views of the disruptive environment in which we now operate indicate the necessity of such moves, and it is imperative to consult and fully engage with the library's customers in this process. Only then will outcomes be acceptable to the whole community that the library serves.

In a recent project with a special library in the social services, the demise of the library was on the cards. A scenario-planning process engaged their whole community and came up with three scenarios. The first described the library much as it was, doing a good job with a mostly print collection and a little digital content. The second imagined the library as completely digital in terms of content delivery, and with a greater focus on developing online information services. The third imagined that the library had reshaped itself to meet the institution's future need for 'knowledge'. This scenario involved developing a Knowledge Centre with the library content and services at its core, but doing much more for the parent organization in terms of capturing and organizing the knowledge of the organization's staff. This is a pertinent illustration of a nimble organization with a smart manager who was determined to talk to her community about what could be. In the end, the second scenario was adopted, together with a firm directive to move as quickly as possible into the third. The example illustrates good management, listening, and engagement with the user community to bring about exciting and imaginative futures.

Speaking the language

There is no doubt that public 'not-for-profit' organizations are not faring well in terms of their finances and their place in the political pecking order. Nor do they have the unquestioned support that they once had across the communities that they serve. They are under threat from political operators who want to minimize the role of government and believe that private enterprise can always do it better. In this maelstrom libraries are not large players, but they are crucially important ones. They have been overtaken by other needs within their user communities and have fallen victims to the increasingly unforgiving process by which the budget pie is divided. If they are to make information available to their user communities, then libraries have to be strong. It remains to be seen what impact the savage financial cuts to the UK's public libraries will have on the communities that they serve. Cuts of up to 25% are harsh. The ideal of the free library service is suffering badly. The literary institutes of the late 19th century were membership organizations funded by subscriptions. How will the public library of the future evolve in different countries? Will it revert to a model from the past?

Libraries can and must demonstrate value on a number of different levels. Value can be demonstrated by stimulating imaginations as to the future nature of the library. It can also be demonstrated in terms of service delivery for an acceptable cost and assessment of the results obtained from that service. Libraries in all sectors now operate in environments that are shaped by the necessity to demonstrate value. They can no longer expect to receive funding as a matter of course, and political support is needed at all levels: user community, library and administration.

It is much more difficult to demonstrate value in a web environment, where the users of digital content often believe that it is just 'free to the net'. The information world is only beginning to work out how it could demonstrate value in this environment. It is also difficult to assess the library's value to its clients when they never actually visit it or do not necessarily understand what it is doing. Many governments are demanding 'efficiency dividends' from their departments, and libraries are not exempt from these enforced savings. Value should be balanced with a tangible, tactile engagement with the communities that are served. The library as an organization is caught between the 'management' and the 'community of users'. This is a powerful position, but one that needs to be managed through the language and needs of both groups.

Professionally adaptable?

Since the beginning of the 21st century the link that had previously existed between the establishment of professional standards and entry into the library profession has suffered significant change. There has been a decline in the membership of professional organizations generally.

The 'library association' is weaker in its capacity to define what the profession requires for membership in the profession. For some time now, employers of librarians have failed to specify in job descriptions a mandated membership of the professional association. They may stipulate that prospective employees should be able to join the association, but not that they should actually be members. A strong profession requires direction from senior, committed members so as to drive its life and growth. These individuals need new ideas and the political will to articulate the future of the profession, and the role of the association in that future.

Whether the association can completely reinvent itself, or even attempt such a vast assignment, remains to be seen. In a period of rapid change any professional association will face serious questions about its role. It will find it hard to be stimulating and engaging and to hold its members together. Thus declining memberships. For some years now, vision statements for the profession issued by some library associations have reflected confusion between holding the membership together and articulating the choice of direction that confronts its members. Such statements have tended to be perspectives on all aspects of the current profession, rather than challenging members' thinking about the future. Those perspectives are more political, even industrial, rather than urging members and non-members to different thinking. This is not a criticism of those associations, but a reflection of the dilemmas that they face.

Final thoughts

Disruptive times are difficult. This is sharply evidenced by companies such as IBM, Nokia and others that have experienced disruptive times and either have failed to re-emerge from the process or have done so in a very diminished state. Mostly, such companies were unable to recognize that the future would not be the same as the past and present in which they had been so successful. They were unable to read the runes and envisage their natural work or business as being done differently by smaller and more nimble 'rivals'. Sticking to the known, core business creates a blindness to perspectives on the periphery. This problem can occur in professions as well as in industries. What are the implications for the skills required of library managers?

In the wake of disruptive digital technologies, the traditional library business model is clearly dead. Certainly, any leader or driver of change needs to avoid being too close to routine library operations and becoming mired or buried in their detail. A wider perspective is imperative. The future skill-set of the librarian includes an ability to deal with ambiguity, conflicting views and uncertainty. Ambiguity, complexity and uncertainty will compromise much of the future operating environment. Working under such conditions will require much forethought and an ability to look outside the library sector and to understand the forces coming into play in the library's future.

Openness to discarding work, skills or outlooks that have been central to the profession is required, retaining only those that are really needed and adopting only what is required to meet the new circumstances. Leaders will understand libraries from the inside, but look at them from the outside, so as to form future-focused perspectives. Truly innovative and customer-focused solutions will be required, so as to ensure that users' information needs can be met. The custodial role around which libraries were built is now largely absent. This is an exciting time to be a professional librarian, and a rare opportunity to create truly new roles for librarians.

The creation of the next iteration of the library profession requires dedicated, insightful work, and sagacity, on the part of both educators and the profession generally, across all sectors. There will be many different approaches and perspectives. We can but welcome the variety of outcomes that will emerge around the globe.

Notes and references

1 Clayton Christenson, www.claytonchristensen.com/key-concepts/.
2 Noble, G. and O'Connor, S., Attitudes Toward Technology as Predictors of Online Catalog Usage, *College and Research Libraries*, **47** (6), November 1986, 605–10.
3 Noble and O'Connor, 1986, 610.
4 www.innocentive.com/.
5 www.innocentive.com/about-innocentive (accessed 1 December 2014).
6 Clayton Christenson, www.claytonchristensen.com/key-concepts/ (accessed 14 June 2014).
7 Clayton Christenson, www.claytonchristensen.com/key-concepts/ (accessed 15 June 2014).
8 Creative Commons licences are designed to enable authors 'to share your knowledge and creativity with the world', http://creativecommons.org/.
9 Artman, J., Motivating Millennials: the next generation of leaders. In Eden, B. L. and Fagan, J. C. (eds), *Leadership in Academic Libraries Today: connecting theory and practice*, Rowman and Littlefield, 2014.

Index